AMERICAN ROOTS

READINGS ON U.S. CULTURAL HISTORY

KAREN BLANCHARD

CHRISTINE ROOT

Longman

American Roots: Readings on U.S. Cultural History

Pearson Education, 10 Bank Street, White Plains, NY 10606

Vice president, director of publishing: Allen Ascher
Editorial director: Louisa Hellegers
Acquisitions editor: Laura Le Dréan
Senior development manager: Penny Laporte
Vice president, director of design and production: Rhea Banker
Associate director of electronic production: Aliza Greenblatt
Executive managing editor: Linda Moser
Production manager: Ray Keating
Production editor: Martin Yu
Senior manufacturing manager: Patrice Fraccio
Senior manufacturing buyer: Dave Dickey
Photo research: Marianne Carello
Cover design: Patricia Wosczyk
Cover credits: Border Gateways: Treasury Department Art Project; Spacewalk: StockTrek/PhotoDisc,
    Inc.; Woman Marching in Suffrage Parade: Corbis; Fireworks at Columbus Celebration: James
    Marshall/Corbis.
Text design: Patricia Wosczyk
Text art: Ron Chironna
Text composition: TSI Graphics
Text credits: see page xii
Photo credits: see page xiii

Library of Congress Cataloging-in-Publication Data

Blanchard, Karen Lourie, 1951–
        American roots: readings on U.S. cultural history / Karen Blanchard, Christine Root.
            p.   cm.
        ISBN 0-201-61995-4 (alk. paper)
            1. United States—Civilization—Problems, exercises, etc.   2. United States—
    History—Problems, exercises, etc.   3. English language—Textbooks for foreign speakers.
    4. Readers—United States.   I. Root, Christine Baker, 1945–   II. Title.

    E169.1.B633   2000
    973'.076—dc21   00-046959

3 4 5 6 7 8 9 10–VHG–05 04 03 02

We dedicate this book to the
Native Americans and immigrants whose hopes, dreams,
cultural traditions, and hard work gave shape to
American Roots

CONTENTS

ACKNOWLEDGMENTS

It is a pleasure to acknowledge our gratitude to several people whose contributions to this book mattered. Many thanks go to Boston College historian Alan Lawson for his generosity and care in reading the manuscript for historical accuracy. In a book like this, photos also tell the story. For their help with photo selection, we thank Sally Pierce and Pamela Greiff at the Boston Athenaeum and Marianne Carello at Pearson Education. We thank our editor, Laura Le Dréan, for taking the idea and running with it.

Big thanks and much love to our parents, Betty Lourie and Stanley Baker for their support, encouragement, and wisdom. To Daniel Blanchard, Jeff Weinstein, and Roberta Steinberg, our thanks for tirelessly researching and critically reviewing articles. And, as always, special thanks to our favorite Roots—David, Matthew, and Ian!

OVERVIEW

To the Teacher

American Roots: Readings on U.S. Cultural History is a reading
skill-builder designed for intermediate students of English as a Second
Language. It is intended to provide a general understanding of the cultural,
social, economic, and political forces that shaped the United States into the
country that we know today. It is a content-based text designed for use in
ESOL adult education programs, colleges, universities, language institutes, and
secondary schools both in the United States and abroad.

American Roots: Readings on U.S. Cultural History is made up of a selection
of authentic readings in a wide variety of writing styles. The articles highlight
people and events notable in the growth and expansion of the United States.
Each article is supported by effective skill-building exercises. The text is based
on the premise that students can read at a higher level than they can produce.
As such, it is designed to help students increase their confidence in reading in
English as well as their understanding of the culture and history of the United
States. Our intention is to help students build the skills necessary for effective
understanding, analysis, and discussion of concepts encountered in these and
future readings. While it is first and foremost a reading text, students also
improve their speaking, listening, and writing skills as they work through the
panoply of written, oral, individual, and collaborative exercises and activities.

In *American Roots* we identify nine broad historical periods and focus on
four or five major events, trends, and/or people within each of those time
periods. The book closes with an epilogue which serves as a link from the past
to the future. While the articles are drawn from authentic sources, we have
taken great care to ensure that the accompanying exercises and activities are
appropriate and manageable for students at the intermediate level.

The basic format for each chapter in *American Roots: Readings on U.S.
Cultural History* is as follows:

▶ Time Line
Each chapter opens with a time line to orient students to the time period.

▶ INTRODUCTION TO THE TIME PERIOD

An overview of the highlights of the historical period sets the scene for the articles in each chapter.

▶ READING

A mixture of short and longer articles, arranged chronologically, illustrates the development of the American national identity that has evolved over time. The articles use important trends and events in American history to portray the values and traits that have characterized the country throughout its history. A short introductory paragraph precedes each article, and maps, photos, charts, and graphs accompany each article as appropriate.

▶ SKILL-BUILDING EXERCISES

Each article is followed by a menu of follow-up exercises to help students expand their vocabulary and strengthen such reading skills as identifying main ideas and details, previewing, scanning, skimming, sequencing, paraphrasing, summarizing, recalling facts, understanding point of view, transitions, and references, as well as separating fact from opinion, examining cause and effect, understanding dashes, and using the dictionary effectively. In addition, students practice exercises such as those found on the TOEFL® test and sharpen their writing skills.

▶ LINKING PAST TO PRESENT/REACT AND RESPOND

Whenever appropriate throughout the text, the connection is made between the past and the way that it has affected the present. Each of these historical links is followed by one or more **React and Respond** questions suitable for oral and/or written follow-through.

▶ HISTORY MAKERS

This activity provides additional writing as well as peer-editing opportunities. Information about an American well known to the historical period of the chapter is provided in list form which students are asked to write into a paragraph.

▶ SKILL REVIEWS

Each chapter concludes with a skill review to provide additional focused practice on a specifically taught skill. The topics of the skill review paragraphs give students additional insight into the time period covered in the chapter.

We hope that you and your students enjoy working together on the readings and exercises in this text and thereby gain a greater understanding of the people, places, and events that are the foundation of *American Roots.*

To the Student

History is important to culture and culture is essential to language. We hope that reading about the history that shaped the cultural behaviors, attitudes, and beliefs of the people of the United States will enrich your study of the English language.

KLB and CBR

CREDITS

TEXT CREDITS

Page 6, from *The United States of America*, by R. Conrad Stein, published in 1996. Reprinted by permission of Children's Press, a division of Grolier Publishing. **Page 13,** based on *America's Story*, by William Jay Jacobs et. al. (Boston: Houghton Mifflin Company, 1990); and *America's Heritage*, by Margaret Stimmann Branson (Lexington, MA: Ginn and Company, 1982). **Page 29,** from *How We Crossed the West: The Adventures of Lewis and Clark*. Copyright © 1997 Rosalyn Schanzer. Published by the National Geographic Society. Reprinted with permission. **Page 32,** adapted from "How Labor Unions Helped Change U.S. History," *Scholastic Update* (February 7, 1986). Copyright © 1986 by Scholastic Inc. Reprinted by permission. **Page 40,** adapted from *The United States in the 19th Century*, by David Rubel. Copyright © 1996 by Scholastic Inc. Reprinted by permission. **Page 43,** adapted from "The Transcendentalists and Their Message," *Cobblestone* (June 1987). © 1987, Cobbleston Publishing Company. Reprinted by permission of the publisher. **Page 53,** adapted from "Entrepreneurs," *Cobblestone* (May 1989). © 1989, Cobbleston Publishing Company. Reprinted by permission of the publisher. **Page 58,** adapted from *The United States in the 19th Century*, by David Rubel. Copyright © 1996 by Scholastic Inc. Reprinted by permission. **Page 62,** adapted from *The United States in the 19th Century*, by David Rubel. Copyright © 1996 by Scholastic Inc. Reprinted by permission. **Page 65,** adapted from *The Young People's History of the United States*, by James Ciment (New York: Barnes & Noble Books, 1998). **Page 81,** adapted from "Women on the Long Prairie," *Scholastic Update* (October 20, 1997). Copyright © 1997 by Scholastic, Inc. Reprinted by permission. **Page 86,** adapted from "Walking the White Road," *Scholastic Update* (November 1, 1996). Copyright © 1996 by Scholastic, Inc. Reprinted by permission. **Page 90,** adapted from "Identity Crisis," *Scholastic Update* (November 17, 1995). Copyright © 1995 by Scholastic, Inc. Reprinted by permission. **Page 101,** adapted from *The United States in the 20th Century*, by David Rubel. Copyright © 1995 by Scholastic Inc. Reprinted by permission. **Page 103,** adapted from *The United States in the 20th Century,* by David Rubel. Copyright © 1995 by Scholastic Inc. Reprinted by permission. **Page 108,** adapted from "The Jazz Sensation," *Cobblestone* (October 1983). © 1983, Cobbleston Publishing Company. Reprinted by permission of the publisher. **Page 113,** adapted from "The Chautauqua Story," *Cobblestone* (July 1984). © 1984, Cobbleston Publishing Company. Reprinted by permission of the publisher. **Page 126,** adapted from "America on Wheels," *Scholastic Update* (February 7, 1997). Copyright © 1997 by Scholastic, Inc. Reprinted by permission. **Page 132,** adapted from "The Harlem Renaissance," *Cobblestone* (February 1991). © 1991, Cobbleston Publishing Company. Reprinted by permission of the publisher. **Page 135,** from *Collected Poems*, by Langston Hughes. Copyright © 1994 by the Estate of Langston Hughes. Reprinted by permission of Alfred A. Knopf, a division of Random House Inc. **Page 137,** adapted from "Rock Bottom," *Scholastic Update* (March 8, 1991). Copyright © 1991 by Scholastic, Inc. Reprinted by permission. **Page 151,** adapted from *The United States in the 20th Century*, by David Rubel. Copyright © 1995 by Scholastic Inc. Reprinted by permission. **Page 154,** Copyright © Blackbirch Graphics, Inc. Published by Twenty-first Century Books, a division of the Millbrook Press, Inc. **Page 159,** Copyright © Blackbirch Graphics, Inc. Published by Twenty-first Century Books, a division of the Millbrook Press, Inc. **Page 171,** adapted from "The Next Frontier," *Scholastic Update* (April 13, 1998). Copyright © 1998 by Scholastic, Inc. Reprinted by permission. **Page 176,** adapted from *The United States in the 20th Century*, by David Rubel. Copyright © 1995 by Scholastic Inc. Reprinted by permission. **Page 187,** adapted from "Long Battle for Women's Equality," *Scholastic Update* (May 18, 1987). Copyright © 1987 by Scholastic, Inc. Reprinted by permission. **Page 197,** © 1999 Time Inc. Reprinted by permission. **Page 204,** from a letter written by Lu Setnika, Public Affairs Director for Patagonia. Reprinted with the permission of Lu Setnika. **Page 208,** © 1997 Time Inc. Reprinted by permission. **Page 212,** © Copyright 1900, Meredith Corporation. All rights reserved. Used with the permission of *Ladies' Home Journal*. **Page 213,** adapted from "Visions of America's Future," *Cobblestone* (January 1984). © 1984, Cobbleston Publishing Company. Reprinted by permission of the publisher. **Page 215,** adapted from "Visions of America's Future," *Cobblestone* (January 1984). © 1984, Cobbleston Publishing Company. Reprinted by permission of the publisher.

PHOTO CREDITS

GETTING TO KNOW EACH OTHER

Each country has a set of characteristics and values that forms its national
identity. As you work through this book, you will discover how the identity
of the United States has been shaped by the dreams of many different people
and by the events in its history.

1. *Put a check (✔) next to the items your country values. Then put a check
next to the things you think are valued in the United States.*

	YOUR COUNTRY	THE UNITED STATES
competition	_____	_____
education	_____	_____
family	_____	_____
freedom	_____	_____
friendship	_____	_____
generosity	_____	_____
hard work	_____	_____
having fun	_____	_____
hospitality	_____	_____
individualism	_____	_____
obedience	_____	_____
privacy	_____	_____
independence	_____	_____
tradition	_____	_____
(other) _____	_____	_____

2. *Which words would you use to describe the people in your culture? Which words would you use to describe Americans?*

	PEOPLE IN YOUR CULTURE	AMERICANS
aggressive	_____	_____
ambitious	_____	_____
creative	_____	_____
flexible	_____	_____
formal	_____	_____
friendly	_____	_____
group-oriented	_____	_____
informal	_____	_____
materialistic	_____	_____
optimistic	_____	_____
passive	_____	_____
practical	_____	_____
reserved	_____	_____
respectful	_____	_____
rigid	_____	_____
time-conscious	_____	_____
(other) _____	_____	_____

3. *Which values and characteristics did you check for both your country and the United States? In small groups, discuss the similarities and differences between the values of your country and those of the United States.*

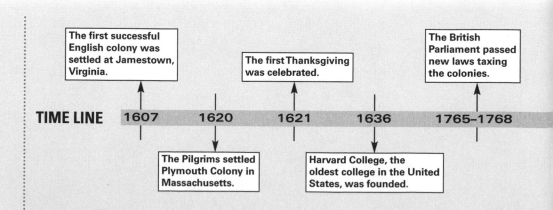

CHAPTER 1

BIRTH OF A NATION

1600–1800

*I*n this chapter, you will learn that the early settlers of the United States were a diverse group of people who valued independence and freedom.

MAKE A CONNECTION
What was happening in your country in the 1600s and 1700s?

The first successful English colony was settled at Jamestown, Virginia.

The first Thanksgiving was celebrated.

The British Parliament passed new laws taxing the colonies.

TIME LINE   1607   1620   1621   1636   1765–1768

The Pilgrims settled Plymouth Colony in Massachusetts.

Harvard College, the oldest college in the United States, was founded.

The Early Years of the United States

Today the United States is a mixture of people, cultures, and ideas from all over the world. The mixing started 500 years ago when European countries began sending explorers to the "New World." By the 1500s, Spain, France, Britain, and several other European countries had established colonies in North America.

Relationships with Native Americans

In the 1500s, North America was a vast wilderness inhabited by various groups of Native Americans. At first, the Native Americans welcomed the colonists and taught them how to hunt, farm, protect themselves from the weather, and use herbs as medicine. The colonists owed much of their early success to help from the Native Americans. Tragically, many Native Americans died in battle with the colonists and from diseases such as smallpox that the colonists brought with them. As time went on, the colonists took over more and more land, forcing the Native Americans to move farther and farther away from their homelands.

Why the Colonists Came to North America

The colonists who settled in North America came from a variety of cultural traditions, and they had many different reasons for leaving their homelands. Some wanted religious or political freedom and the freedom to express

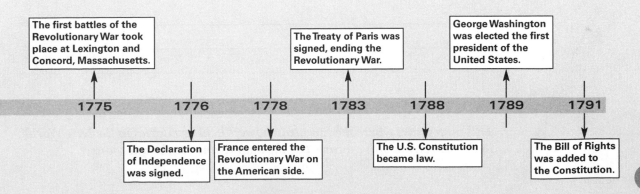

The first battles of the Revolutionary War took place at Lexington and Concord, Massachusetts.

The Treaty of Paris was signed, ending the Revolutionary War.

George Washington was elected the first president of the United States.

1775   1776   1778   1783   1788   1789   1791

The Declaration of Independence was signed.

France entered the Revolutionary War on the American side.

The U.S. Constitution became law.

The Bill of Rights was added to the Constitution.

themselves without fear. Others came because they wanted to own land, which they could not do in Europe. Still others were excited by the adventure of moving to a new part of the world. However, not everyone came freely. About 350,000 Africans were brought to North America and sold as slaves. More than anyone else, the English colonists first shaped the character of the United States. They brought their language, institutions, values, and customs with them.

The Separation from Great Britain

By the mid-1700s, Great Britain had established thirteen colonies along the Atlantic coast of North America, from New Hampshire to Georgia. For many years, the colonists lived quite happily under British rule. But by 1764, serious disagreements between the colonies and the British government had developed. The main problem was that the colonies wanted more independence, but Britain wanted more control. The colonists especially disliked the heavy taxes they had to pay to Britain. The situation got worse, and in 1776, the colonists declared their independence from Britain. The American Revolution began.

Answer the questions.

1. What are some reasons that people came to the New World?

   a. _____

   b. _____

   c. _____

   d. _____

   e. _____

2. Where did Britain establish her thirteen colonies?

   _____

   _____

   _____

3. What was the main problem between the colonies and Britain during the 1700s?

   _____

   _____

   _____

BUILD YOUR MAP-READING SKILLS

This map shows where the European powers held territories in the New World in the late eighteenth century. Use the map to answer the questions.

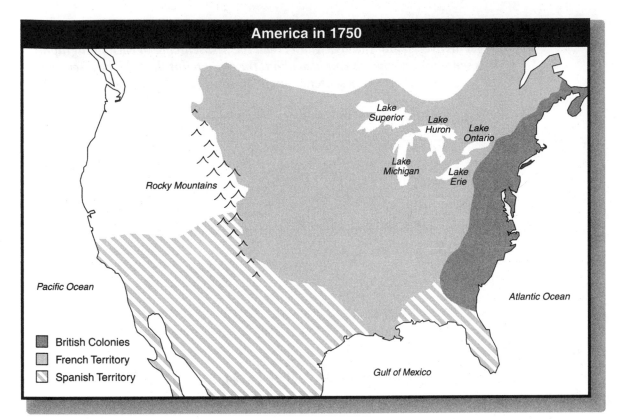

America in 1750

Lake Superior
Lake Huron
Lake Ontario
Lake Michigan
Lake Erie

Rocky Mountains

Pacific Ocean

Atlantic Ocean

Gulf of Mexico

- ☐ British Colonies
- ☐ French Territory
- ☐ Spanish Territory

18th

1. In the late <u>eighteenth</u> century, which European countries owned territories in the New World?

_____

2. Which European country owned the largest territory in what is now the United States?

_____

3. Which European country owned Florida?

_____

CULTURE KERNEL

The oldest city in the United States, St. Augustine, Florida, was established in 1565 by the Spanish.

READING 1 Colonial America

The first successful British colony was founded in 1607. During the next 125 years, Britain established twelve more colonies along the east coast of North America. Life in the thirteen British colonies differed from region to region. In the New England and Middle Atlantic colonies, the economy was based on small businesses, trade, and small farms. In contrast, the southern colonies developed a plantation economy that was dependent on slavery. In this article, you will read about some of the problems and successes of the early British colonists.

BEFORE YOU READ

To get an overview of the article, first read the first sentence of each paragraph. This sentence will give you an idea about the main point that will be discussed in the paragraph. Write each sentence on the lines provided. Then read the article.

1. _____

_____

2. _____

_____

3. _____

_____

4. _____

_____

Colonial America

1   England emerged as the dominant colonial power in the present-day United States by the mid-1700s. Thirteen English colonies, with 1.3 million settlers, stretched along the Atlantic from New Hampshire south to Georgia. At that time, about 200,000 slaves lived in the colonies, mostly in the South. Other colonial powers, such as the French, the Spanish, and the Dutch, had smaller settlements in North America.

2   Most English colonists were hard-working, thrifty people who made the long, dangerous Atlantic voyage because of the promises America offered. Land in

Daily life in colonial times

the colonies was cheap, and the soil was fertile. The possibility existed for a free man to arrive on American shores penniless and become a prosperous farmer within a few years. No other place on earth offered an Englishman such rapid opportunities for advancement.

3   From the beginning, settlers established a form of democracy in the English colonies. Sheriffs and other township officers were elected. The New England colonies had meetings to discuss community projects such as road building and bridge construction. Yet large classes of people were excluded from this democratic process. Voting was limited to free adult males who owned property. Women, slaves, and the very poor had no vote.

4   Colonial life was a mixture of trials and triumphs. The greatest danger the farming communities faced was epidemics of diseases such as smallpox and yellow fever. Doctors were rare in colonial America, and sick people were nursed with teas made from roots and herbs. In villages, weddings were gigantic feasts that sometimes lasted two or three days. For recreation, colonial men raced horses, while groups of women talked together and stitched blankets in "quilting bees." Most colonists were deeply religious, and much of their social activity revolved around the church.

CHECK YOUR COMPREHENSION

Circle the letter of the choice that best completes each sentence.

1. In the mid-1700s, the French, Spanish, and Dutch had _____.
   a. sent over 2,000 slaves to the colonies
   b. small settlements in North America
   c. thirteen colonies along the Atlantic coast
   d. abandoned their colonies in America

2. English people came to America because _____.
   a. it offered rapid opportunities for advancement
   b. colonial life was full of trials
   c. the voyage was dangerous
   d. they enjoyed horse racing and quilting bees

3. The greatest danger farming communities faced was _____.
   a. infertile land
   b. poor transportation systems
   c. religious fanaticism
   d. epidemics of disease

4. _____ were allowed to participate in the democratic process in the colonies.
   a. Free adult men
   b. Rich women
   c. Adult slaves
   d. Very poor men

5. For recreation, colonial men _____.
  a. farmed the fertile land
  b. raced horses
  c. made blankets
  d. nursed the sick

BUILD YOUR READING SKILLS: Recognizing Main Ideas

The most important skill good readers need to develop is the ability to recognize main ideas. English writing is divided into paragraphs. Each paragraph is usually about one topic, which is the main idea of the paragraph. The main idea of the paragraph is often (but not always) stated in a sentence called the *topic sentence.* Identifying the topic sentences of the paragraphs in an article will help you recognize the main ideas. The topic sentence of a paragraph is usually the first sentence. As you saw in Reading 1, the topic sentence of each of the four paragraphs is the first sentence.

Read the list of main points from the article. Write the number of the paragraph that discusses each point.

_2_ **a.** why British colonists came to America

_3_ **b.** government in the British colonies

_4_ **c.** problems and successes of colonial life

_1_ **d.** the size and location of the thirteen British colonies

BUILD YOUR READING SKILLS: Understanding Details

You just learned that a paragraph is usually about one topic called the main idea, which is often stated in the topic sentence. What about the rest of the sentences in the paragraph? What is their purpose? The other sentences in a paragraph give details to support or explain the main idea.

Below is a list of details the author uses to support the main topics in Reading 1. Write each supporting detail under the appropriate topic on page 9.

  a. Land in the colonies was fertile.

  b. Diseases such as smallpox and yellow fever killed many settlers.

  c. Thirteen British colonies were established along the Atlantic coast.

  d. Doctors were rare in the colonies.

  e. Land in the colonies was cheap.

  f. Leaders were elected by the people.

  g. Other colonial powers such as France and Spain had smaller settlements.

  h. Settlers could become prosperous farmers quickly.

  i. The colonists developed recreation such as horse racing and quilting bees.

j. There were 1.3 million English settlers.

k. Town meetings were held to discuss community projects.

l. Women, slaves, and poor people could not vote.

1. England was the dominant colonial power in the United States by the mid-1700s.

_____ c g _____

_____

_____

2. Most English colonists came to America because of the promises it offered.

_____ a e h _____

_____

_____

3. The people established a form of democracy in the English colonies.

_____ f _____

_____

_____

4. Colonial life was a mixture of trials and triumphs.

_____ b d i _____

_____

_____

EXPAND YOUR VOCABULARY

Match each word from the reading with its synonym.

_____ 1. dominant	a. combination
_____ 2. prosperous	b. huge
_____ 3. rapid	c. uncommon
_____ 4. excluded	d. most important
_____ 5. mixture	e. frugal
_____ 6. triumph	f. wealthy
_____ 7. rare	g. fast
_____ 8. gigantic	h. achievement
_____ 9. trials	i. left out
_____10. thrifty	j. difficulties

TALK ABOUT IT

What was life in the New World like for the colonists? What kinds of problems did they face? What did they do for recreation?

 LINKING PAST TO PRESENT The rebellious spirit of the colonists gave birth to the strong sense of independence that still characterizes the people of the United States today. Americans value their independence and like to rely on themselves instead of others. Many young Americans move out of their parents' houses when they graduate from high school or college because they want to feel independent. Parents often encourage financial and emotional independence in their children.

REACT AND RESPOND Is it common for young people in your country to move out of their parents' houses before they get married? Why or why not? Do parents in your country encourage financial and emotional independence in their children?

CULTURE KERNEL

Until the early 1700s, the person who received a letter was the one who had to pay for the stamp.

WRITE ABOUT IT

Pretend that you were a settler in one of the thirteen original colonies. On a separate piece of paper, write a letter to a friend or relative back home describing your new life. Write about your work and recreation. Discuss your hopes, dreams, and problems.

BUILD YOUR READING SKILLS: Understanding How to Scan

We read for several different reasons. We also read in different ways. Sometimes we read something quickly in order to find a specific piece of information. This is called scanning.

Scan the chart to answer the following questions. Then look at the map on page 12 to see where the thirteen original colonies were located.

1. In what year was Rhode Island founded? _____

2. Which was the first colony? _____

3. How many middle colonies were there? _____

4. Which colony was founded in order to give religious freedom to Catholics?

   _____

5. Which colony was founded in 1733? _____

6. How many colonies were founded for the purpose of trade?

_____

7. What colony was founded for people who had debts? _____

8. Why was New Hampshire founded? _____

COLONY CHART		
COLONY	**DATE FOUNDED**	**REASON FOUNDED**
The New England Colonies		
Massachusetts	1620	Religious freedom for Protestants
New Hampshire	1630	Political, religious, and economic freedom
Connecticut	1636	Religious freedom
Rhode Island	1636	Religious freedom
The Middle Colonies		
New York	1626	Trade
Maryland	1634	Religious freedom for Catholics
Delaware	1638	Trade
New Jersey	1664	Trade
Pennsylvania	1681	Religious freedom for Quakers
The Southern Colonies		
Virginia	1607	Trade
North Carolina	1653	Trade
South Carolina	1670	Trade
Georgia	1733	Colony for people who had debts

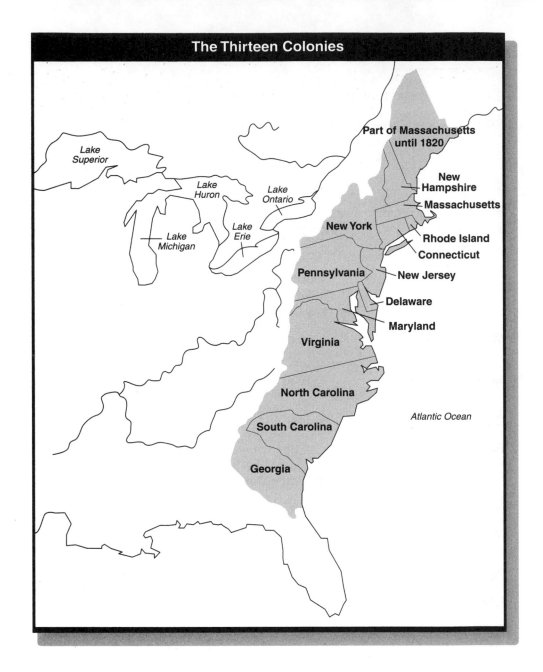

The Thirteen Colonies

Lake Superior

Lake Huron

Lake Ontario

Lake Erie

Lake Michigan

Part of Massachusetts until 1820

New Hampshire

Massachusetts

New York

Rhode Island

Connecticut

Pennsylvania

New Jersey

Delaware

Maryland

Virginia

North Carolina

Atlantic Ocean

South Carolina

Georgia

READING 2 **John Peter Zenger: Pioneer of the Free Press**

As far back as colonial times, freedom of expression was valued. Most colonists believed they should be allowed to express themselves even if it was to criticize the government. In this article, you will read about an important legal case that helped to establish freedom of the press in America.

John Peter Zenger: Pioneer of the Free Press

1   Americans today believe strongly in freedom of the press—the right of newspaper or magazine publishers to print what they want. In colonial times, however, the royal governors held power over the press. Anyone who dared to write critically about government officials might be charged with libel—printing statements that unfairly harm a person's reputation.

2   In 1735, John Peter Zenger, publisher of the *New York Weekly Journal,* was arrested for libeling the governor. After spending almost twelve months in jail, Zenger finally came to trial. Zenger's lawyer made a brilliant defense. He said that Zenger had been speaking and writing the truth. Certainly, the lawyer insisted, it was no crime to speak and write the truth! The jury agreed and set Zenger free, while the onlookers in the courtroom cheered.

3   Zenger's trial is important in history for two reasons. First, it showed that while people can be punished for libel, they cannot be punished for telling or printing the truth. Second, it marked a big step toward freedom of the press in America.

BUILD YOUR TEST-TAKING SKILLS

You will see this type of exercise throughout the book. It provides you practice in taking standardized tests. Circle the letter of the choice that best completes each sentence.

1. The article mainly discusses _____.
   a. the actions of the governor of New York
   b. Zenger's time in jail
   c. Zenger's court case
   d. the *New York Weekly Journal*

2. According to the author, Zenger's court case _____.
   a. was an important victory for freedom of the press
   b. was an insignificant event
   c. never should have come to trial
   d. is an example of libel

3. It can be concluded from the article that the author _____.
   a. disapproved of Zenger's lawyer
   b. thinks freedom of the press should be limited
   c. likes Zenger's style of writing
   d. supports freedom of the press

4. The word *libel* in the third sentence of the first paragraph means
_____.
   a. writing false accusations
   b. writing critically about government officials
   c. printing statements that unfairly harm a person's reputation
   d. power over the press

5. The word *he* in the fourth sentence of the second paragraph refers to
_____.
   a. John Peter Zenger
   b. Zenger's lawyer
   c. the governor of New York
   d. the jury

6. The main purpose of the article is to _____.
   a. provide a short history of important court cases
   b. show the differences between colonial and modern times
   c. give a biography of John Peter Zenger
   d. describe the impact of the Zenger case on freedom of the press

READING 3 Documents That Shaped the United States

The previous readings in this book have described life in colonial times and told you a little about the people who founded the United States. This reading contains information about three documents that were very important to the creation and development of the United States. Knowing the basic ideas in these documents will help you understand the ideals that the founders wanted for the new country and the kinds of laws and government that they wanted to pass on to future generations.

BEFORE YOU READ

1. Look over the reading. Write the names of the three documents on the lines provided.

   a. _____

   b. _____

   c. _____

2. Has your country ever declared its independence from another country? What country? When?

3. Does your country have a constitution? When was it written? What are the basic ideas in it? Have the original ideas been changed over the years?

The Declaration of Independence (July 4, 1776)

By 1776, the colonists realized that they needed to separate from Great Britain. On July 4, the colonists broke all their ties with England by issuing their Declaration of Independence. The thirteen colonies immediately became thirteen American states. The main author of the Declaration of Independence was Thomas Jefferson, a lawyer and farmer from Virginia who later became the third president. Two of the most important ideas expressed in the Declaration of Independence are that "all men are created equal" and that they are entitled to "life, liberty, and the pursuit of happiness." The belief in equality for all is central to the idea of democracy in the United States. Although not everyone in the United States has always enjoyed equal rights, the idea of equality stated in the Declaration of Independence has inspired generations of people to fight for their rights and be tolerant of others.

On March 5, 1770, a crowd of people in Boston began making fun of British soldiers. The soldiers fired their guns, and five colonists were killed. The incident was called the Boston Massacre and soon became a symbol of British cruelty.

The Constitution of the United States (1788)

After the United States won its independence from Britain, Americans faced a new challenge. The thirteen new states needed to find a way to work together as one country. Using principles from the Declaration of Independence, the Founding Fathers* wrote the document that still forms the basis of the U.S. government—the Constitution. The Constitution describes the organization of the national government. It divides the government into three branches:

- The legislative branch is called the Congress. Its function is to make the laws for the country.
- The executive branch is headed by the president. It enforces laws made by Congress and controls the nation's military and foreign policy.
- The judicial branch is headed by the Supreme Court. The Supreme Court interprets the laws that Congress passes and makes sure that they are compatible with the Constitution.

The Founding Fathers wanted to be certain that no one branch of government had more power than the other two. They established a system of checks and balances, in which each branch of government has some power over the other two. In 1788, the Constitution of the United States became law, and in 1789, George Washington was elected the first president.

The Bill of Rights (1791)

After the Constitution was approved, many citizens were concerned that it created a strong national government but did not protect the basic rights of people. As a result, ten amendments, or additions, were added to the Constitution. These amendments are called the Bill of Rights. The Bill of Rights guarantees personal rights such as freedom of religion, freedom of speech, freedom of the press, and a fair trial in court. The rights protected in the First Amendment form the cornerstone of American democracy. This was the first time that a country wrote a constitution that promised to protect the individual civil and political rights of all its free citizens. At that time, however, *citizens* referred only to white males. Women and blacks, for example, were not considered citizens.

---

*__Founding Fathers__ writers of the Constitution

CHECK YOUR COMPREHENSION

Match each term from the reading with its definition.

_____ 1. Declaration of Independence

_____ 2. legislative branch

_____ 3. Bill of Rights

_____ 4. the Constitution

_____ 5. judicial branch

_____ 6. checks and balances

_____ 7. executive branch

_____ 8. amendment

_____ 9. democracy

a. branch of government that interprets the laws

b. system that controls power among the three branches of government

c. document that expresses the idea of equality for all

d. branch of government that makes the laws

e. any addition to the Constitution

f. document that forms the basis of the U.S. government

g. branch of government that enforces the laws

h. document guaranteeing the personal rights of citizens

i. government created by the people

EXPAND YOUR VOCABULARY

Answer each of the questions yes *or* no.

1. If you are entitled to a two-week vacation, should your boss refuse to let you go? _____

2. If the post office guarantees that a letter will arrive in three days, should you be upset if it takes a week? _____

3. If a law is enforced, should you ignore it? _____

4. If you don't accept anything new or different, are you tolerant? _____

5. If you value something, would you throw it away? _____

6. If you are certain about something, do you question it? _____

TALK ABOUT IT

You have read that the Supreme Court interprets the laws that Congress passes and decides whether or not they agree with the Constitution. Sometimes the decisions of the Supreme Court are controversial. Read about the legal cases on page 18 and decide whether or not you agree with the decisions the Supreme Court made.

1. The First Amendment guarantees freedom of speech, even speech that some people find offensive. This means Americans must sometimes accept unpopular speech in order to preserve the spirit of the freedom. The Supreme Court determines what types of speech are covered by the First Amendment. It defined "speech" to be both spoken words and symbolic speech.

   In the 1960s, some people began burning the American flag as an expression of protest against the government. This angered people who felt that the flag is a symbol of the United States and should be protected. In response, Congress passed the Flag Protection Act in 1989, which made it illegal to burn or destroy a U.S. flag. However, in 1990, the Court ruled that the Flag Protection Act was unconstitutional. It decided that the burning of the American flag is an example of "symbolic speech" and is therefore protected by the First Amendment. What do you think?

2. The Internet has caused much controversy on the subject of free speech. In the 1990s, many people became angry about the amount of material on the Internet that is not appropriate for children. As a result, Congress passed a law that made it illegal to send or show inappropriate material to people under the age of eighteen. In 1997, the Supreme Court ruled that the law was unconstitutional. The Court said that freedom of speech applies to the Internet, and since it is impossible to tell the age of people using the Internet, the law would violate the rights of adults on the Internet. What do you think?

3. The First Amendment also states that religion and the government must be separated. However, for many years schoolchildren began each day with a prayer. In fact, in some states a prayer was required by law. In 1961, a group of parents in New York sued the Department of Education because they thought it was unfair to make students say a prayer in school. The lower courts ruled against the parents and said it was legal for New York to allow prayer in school as long as no student was forced to participate. The question then came before the Supreme Court: Does a voluntary prayer said in public schools violate the First Amendment's separation of religion and government? The Supreme Court decided that all prayer, even voluntary prayer, in public schools was unconstitutional. What do you think?

BUILD YOUR DICTIONARY SKILLS

Dictionaries give a lot of useful information about words. Every new entry in the dictionary is written in bold print. It shows the correct spelling of the word. Look at the information for the word *function* taken from a dictionary:

function[1] /ˈfʌŋkʃən/ *n* **1** the usual purpose of a thing, or the job that someone usually does: *What's **the** exact **function** of this program?* | *A manager has to **perform** many different **functions**.* **2** a large party or ceremonial event, especially for an important or official occasion: *The mayor has to attend all kinds of official functions.*
function[2] *v* [I] to work in a particular way or in the correct way: *Can you explain exactly how this new system will function?*

A. *Use a dictionary to correct these misspelled words. If a word is spelled correctly, write **C** on the line.*

1. citisen _____

2. gigantic _____

3. dominent _____

4. foundation _____

5. interpert _____

6. foriegn _____

The dictionary also shows how to pronounce words. It tells where to divide a word into syllables and which syllable to stress when you say the word. A dot separates the syllables.

B. *Use a dictionary to divide these words from the chapter into syllables. Include the stress mark.*

1. liberty _____

2. revolutionary _____

3. libel _____

4. independence _____

5. publisher _____

6. equality _____

7. guarantee _____

8. democracy _____

9. dominant _____

10. tolerant _____

HISTORY MAKER: Benjamin Franklin

Read about Benjamin Franklin, one of the most famous and respected people in American history.

The name Benjamin Franklin should be included on any list of the greatest Americans. Franklin was born in 1706 in Boston, Massachusetts, and died in 1790 in Philadelphia, Pennsylvania. One of seventeen children, Franklin was a writer, printer, inventor, scientist, and diplomat. He was one of the men who signed the Declaration of Independence, and it was Franklin who persuaded the French to help the colonists in the American Revolution. In addition to his political activities, he discovered that lightning is a form of electricity and then invented the lightening rod to save buildings from fires caused by lightning. He went on to invent bifocal eyeglasses

Ben Franklin discovers lightning is a form of electricity.

and the Franklin stove, which gave more heat than other stoves of the time and used less fuel. Franklin also started the first public library, the first fire department, and the first insurance company. His face appears on postage stamps and on the $100 bill. He is also known for the collection of proverbs he wrote and published, *Poor Richard's Almanack.*

TALK ABOUT IT

Poor Richard's Almanack reflects Franklin's philosophy that thrift and hard work are the keys to success. *Poor Richard's Almanack* was one of the most popular books available and greatly influenced American thought both before and after the Revolutionary War.

A. *Here are some of the proverbs from* Poor Richard's Almanack. *Read and discuss the meanings of the proverbs. Do you have any similar proverbs in your language?*

1. Lost time is never found.

2. God helps those who help themselves.

3. Haste makes waste.

4. A penny saved is a penny earned.

5. Early to bed and early to rise makes a man healthy, wealthy, and wise.

6. Fish and guests stink after three days.

7. Three people can keep a secret if two of them are dead.

8. If you cannot follow, you cannot lead.

9. Be careful of your money; a small leak will sink a big ship.

B. *Choose one of the proverbs in the previous exercise and explain why it has meaning in your life.*

LINKING PAST TO PRESENT The colonists believed in hard work. They did not believe in wasting time or money. Americans today are very time-conscious and money-conscious. They still believe that the real key to success lies in working hard.

REACT AND RESPOND What examples can you think of that show Americans are time-conscious and money-conscious? Would you consider the people of your country to be very time-conscious? Are they money-conscious?

HISTORY MAKER: George Washington

Carefully read the list of facts about another history maker, George Washington, the first president of the United States. Then choose the information you want from the list to write a paragraph about him on a separate piece of paper. Refer to the paragraph on Benjamin Franklin on page 19 as a guide for writing your own **History Makers** *throughout this book. Be sure to begin your paragraph with a topic sentence that states the main idea.*

The signing of the United States constitution

- remembered as "Father of His Country"
- born in 1732 in Virginia
- attended only seven years of school
- was one of the most important leaders in U.S. history
- played important role in gaining independence for the American colonies
- created the Continental Army, which fought and won the American Revolution
- was unanimously elected the first president of the United States in 1789
- helped write the Constitution
- laid down the guidelines for future presidents
- was known for his honesty and strong character
- died in 1799

Exchange your paragraph with a partner. Read your partner's paragraph and check it for correct grammar, punctuation, and capitalization.

SKILL REVIEW: Scanning

Thanksgiving is one of the most important holidays in the United States. Scan the passage to find answers to the questions.

1. Where was the first Thanksgiving celebrated? _____

2. When was the first Thanksgiving celebration held? _____

3. When is Thanksgiving celebrated now? _____

4. What president changed the date of Thanksgiving to the last Thursday in November? _____

5. When did Congress make the fourth Thursday in November the legal date of Thanksgiving? _____

A Thanksgiving feast in colonial times

Thanksgiving

1   Thanksgiving is a holiday in the United States that is always celebrated on the fourth Thursday in November. It is a time when families come from near and far to be together for a big dinner and to give thanks for all the good things in their lives.

2   The first Thanksgiving celebration in the United States was held in Virginia in December 1619. It was a religious day of giving thanks to God and did not include food. Two years later, the first Thanksgiving in the New England colonies was celebrated a few months after the Pilgrims arrived in Plymouth, Massachusetts. Many of the Pilgrims had died during the long,

cold Massachusetts winter, but summer had brought new hope and a spirit of optimism to the colonists. They decided to have a festival in the autumn to thank God for the success of their corn harvest. The festival lasted three days and included the traditional foods such as turkey and pumpkin that we still eat today on Thanksgiving Day.

3   Although Thanksgiving has always been celebrated in the autumn after the harvest, it has not always been celebrated on the same date. In 1789, President George Washington named November 26 as a day of national thanksgiving. In 1863, President Abraham Lincoln changed the date of Thanksgiving to the last Thursday in November. In 1939, President Franklin D. Roosevelt made the date one week earlier. The time between Thanksgiving and Christmas was the biggest shopping period of the year, and he wanted to help businesses by giving people another week for shopping. In 1941, Congress made the fourth Thursday in November the legal date of Thanksgiving.

PUT IT TOGETHER

Discuss the questions.

1. The first Independence Day celebration in the United States took place on July 4, 1777. Today, most communities around the country still celebrate Independence Day with parades and firework displays. Does your country have an independence holiday? If so, how do you celebrate it?

2. Thomas Jefferson wrote in the Declaration of Independence that "all men are created equal" and in its first draft specifically criticized slavery. When he was president, Jefferson supported the movement to stop slave importation. However, as a plantation owner, he owned many slaves. Since Jefferson argued against slavery, do you think it was right for him to keep slaves?

3. Does your country have a harvest holiday like Thanksgiving? If so, how do you celebrate it?

CHAPTER 2

A GROWING NATION

The Early 1800s

*I*n this chapter, you will learn that the early 1800s was a time of change and growth for the United States.

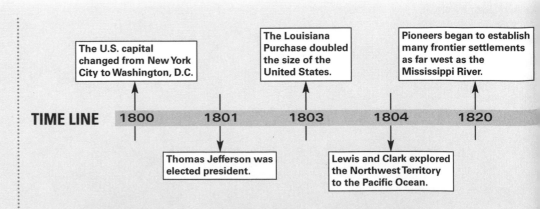

┌╌╌ **MAKE A CONNECTION** ┊
└╌╌ What was happening in your country at the beginning of the nineteenth century?

TIME LINE

| 1800 | 1801 | 1803 | 1804 | 1820 |

The U.S. capital changed from New York City to Washington, D.C.

The Louisiana Purchase doubled the size of the United States.

Pioneers began to establish many frontier settlements as far west as the Mississippi River.

Thomas Jefferson was elected president.

Lewis and Clark explored the Northwest Territory to the Pacific Ocean.

The United States in the Early 1800s

In the first half of the nineteenth century, the newly independent country changed in many ways.

Expansion into the West

The United States more than doubled its size with the purchase of the Louisiana Territory from France. The adventurous spirit of many people led to the exploration of this and other new territories. As they moved west, settlers fought bitter wars with Native Americans, whose ancestors had lived there for thousands of years. Over time, most of the Native Americans were killed or forced off their lands.

As more people moved west, trade increased and cities grew. By 1820, there were settlements as far as the Mississippi River. By the 1830s, there were settlements up to the Rocky Mountains, and by the 1840s, the Far West was becoming settled.

Industrialization in the Northeast

Before the 1800s, the United States had been mainly a nation of farmers. But during the first half of the nineteenth century, the Northeast became industrialized. The number of factories multiplied, and the Northeast became

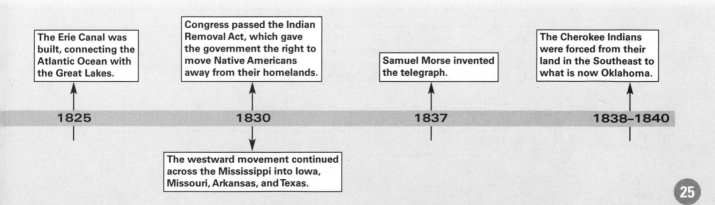

The Erie Canal was built, connecting the Atlantic Ocean with the Great Lakes.

Congress passed the Indian Removal Act, which gave the government the right to move Native Americans away from their homelands.

Samuel Morse invented the telegraph.

The Cherokee Indians were forced from their land in the Southeast to what is now Oklahoma.

1825   **1830**   **1837**   **1838–1840**

The westward movement continued across the Mississippi into Iowa, Missouri, Arkansas, and Texas.

the center of manufacturing. The growing population and the arrival of new immigrants provided workers for the factories. During this same time, transportation improved greatly. Roads were built to link cities and towns, and canals were dug to link lakes and rivers.

Cotton Production in the South

While industry was expanding in the North, cotton cultivation was spreading in the South. New technologies made growing cotton easier and more profitable. As a result, more cotton was grown and the use of slave labor increased greatly. Life for slaves on southern plantations was cruel and hard. In the North, there was much opposition to slavery, and by the early 1800s, all the northern states had banned slavery. The economy of the southern states, however, continued to depend on slaves as a source of cheap labor.

Social Reform

As the country expanded, it became clear that many Americans did not enjoy the rights guaranteed to them in the Declaration of Independence and Constitution. Some people wanted to make changes, or reforms. Many reformers wanted to end slavery. Other reformers worked to get equal rights for women, such as the right to vote. Still others demanded better schools for all children. The reform movements reflected the belief of many Americans that life can always be made better.

Answer the questions.

1. What happened to the Native Americans as settlers moved west?

   _____

   _____

2. How did the economy in the North change?

   _____

   _____

3. How was the economy in the South dependent on slavery?

   _____

   _____

4. What changes did the reformers demand?

   a. _____

   b. _____

   c. _____

The Adventures of Lewis and Clark

One of Thomas Jefferson's greatest accomplishments as president of the United States was the purchase of the Louisiana Territory from France. Jefferson asked Congress for money to explore the new territory. This article describes the exploration of this territory. It also includes excerpts from the journals of some of the explorers.

BEFORE YOU READ

Study the map that shows the growth of the United States and the route Lewis and Clark took. Then answer the questions on page 28.

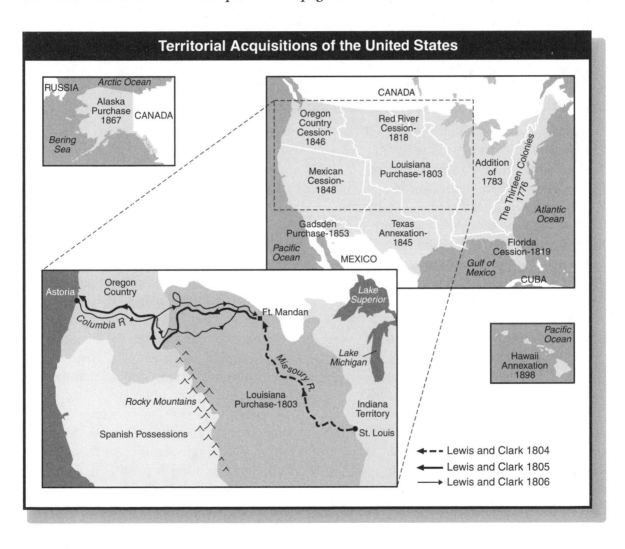

Territorial Acquisitions of the United States

RUSSIA
Arctic Ocean
Alaska Purchase 1867
CANADA
Bering Sea

CANADA
Oregon Country Cession- 1846
Red River Cession- 1818
Mexican Cession- 1848
Louisiana Purchase-1803
Addition of 1783
The Thirteen Colonies 1776
Atlantic Ocean
Gadsden Purchase-1853
Texas Annexation- 1845
Pacific Ocean
MEXICO
Florida Cession-1819
Gulf of Mexico
CUBA

Astoria
Oregon Country
Columbia R.
Ft. Mandan
Lake Superior
Missouri R.
Lake Michigan
Rocky Mountains
Louisiana Purchase-1803
Indiana Territory
Spanish Possessions
St. Louis

Pacific Ocean
Hawaii Annexation 1898

◄- - - Lewis and Clark 1804
◄——— Lewis and Clark 1805
———► Lewis and Clark 1806

1. In what year did the United States make the Louisiana Purchase?

   _____

2. What were the eastern and western boundaries of the addition in 1783?

   _____

3. What was the most recent addition to the United States? _____

4. In what year did the United States acquire Florida? _____

5. What territory did the United States acquire in 1848? _____

The Adventures of Lewis and Clark

1   In 1803, the United States purchased the Louisiana Territory from France, which doubled its size. Within a year, President Thomas Jefferson had the money and support from Congress that he needed to send a small group of people to explore _-2_ this huge new territory. Jefferson called the group the Corps of Discovery. He asked his personal secretary, Meriwether Lewis, to lead the corps. Lewis chose his friend William Clark to accompany him on what was to be one of the greatest adventure stories in America's history.

2   Jefferson believed that there was an all-water route that linked the Atlantic and Pacific Oceans. He wanted Lewis and Clark to find this route so that Americans could settle the West. He also wanted them to find out what kinds of people, plants, and animals were there. Led by Lewis and Clark, the Corps of Discovery left St. Louis, Missouri, on May 14, 1804, to explore the new territory that was west of the Mississippi River.

3   Although they never found a direct water route, Lewis and Clark accomplished a great deal during their twenty-eight-month-long expedition. They traveled through 7,689 miles (12,400 kilometers) of wilderness to the Pacific Ocean and back, making detailed maps of prairies, mountains, rivers, and forests. The men faced and overcame many dangers during their trip, including bear attacks and harsh weather. Sometimes they were so hungry that they ate their horses. Despite the hardships, they returned with valuable information about the climate and geography of the territory. They discovered many plants and animals that had previously been unknown to science. The corps made peaceful contact with many Indians. They learned about the customs and languages of more than fifty Indian nations living in the region. Perhaps their most important contribution to history, however, was that they opened the West to settlers and fur traders. The success of their work helped make the settlement of the western frontier possible.

BUILD YOUR READING SKILLS: Recognizing Main Ideas

Check (✓) the topics that are discussed in Reading 1.

_____ 1. how Lewis and Clark prepared for their expedition

_____ 2. the reasons President Jefferson sent Lewis and Clark on an expedition

_____ 3. some problems Lewis and Clark encountered on their trip

_____ 4. the types of plants and animals that live in the Louisiana Territory

_____ 5. the accomplishments of the expedition

_____ 6. the most important contribution the corps made

We can learn much about the Lewis and Clark expedition by reading the journals the men kept. Because these journals were written 200 years ago, some of the language is old-fashioned, and some of the vocabulary is hard.

Read these short journal excerpts and do the exercises that follow. As you read, do not worry about understanding every word. Read for the main idea.

October 24, 1804

A Mr. Toussaint Charbonneau came down to see us, and wished to be hired as an interpreter. This man has a wife called Sacagawea, who is about 14 or 15 years of age. She is from the Shoshoni [Snake] nation and was captured by Hidatsa Indians when she was about 10. The Shoshonis live by the Rocky Mountains and own many horses. Charbonneau informs us that his squaw will tell these Indians of our need for horses to carry baggage over the mountains. She is with child. [Other member of expedition]

October 24, 1804

We saw one of the Grand Chiefs of the Mandan Indians out hunting. With great cordiality we smoked the [peace] pipe. Every day curious men, women, and children flocked down to see us. These are the most friendly Indians inhabiting the Missouri. [Clark]

Homework Wednesday

May 14, 1805

In the evening, the men discovered a large brown [grizzly] bear, and six hunters went out to attack him. Each put a bullet through him, two through both lungs. In an instant this monster ran at them with open mouth. Two more men shot him, but this stopped his motion for a moment only. The men ran for the river and the bear pursued.

The bear was so close that the men threw aside their guns and threw themselves into the river, though the bank was 20 feet high. The animal plunged into the water a few feet behind the second man. One of those still on shore shot the bear through the head and finally killed him. [*Lewis*]

June 27, 1805

Hail about the size of pigeons' eggs covered the ground to one inch and a half. As the balls struck the ground they would rebound to the height of 20 or 30 feet before they touched again. If one had struck a man on the naked head, it would have killed him. The men saved themselves by getting under a canoe. [*Clark*]

August 30, 1805

Traversed some of the worst roads that a horse ever passed on the sides of steep and stony mountains, some covered with snow. . . . Several times compelled to kill a colt for our men and selves to eat for want of meat. Encamped one night at a bold running creek which I named Hungry Creek as we had nothing to eat. [*Clark*]

Woke this morning and to our great surprise we were covered with snow. Our moccasins froze; the ink freezes in my pen. [*Other member of expedition*]

October 5, 1805

I went on shore and found the Indians much frightened in their lodges. They thought we were not men but birds that fell from the clouds. As soon as they saw Sacagawea, they understood our friendly intentions, as no woman ever accompanies a war party. [*Clark*]

Homework due Wednesday.

November 7, 1805

We were encamped under a high hill when the morning fog cleared off. Ocean in view! Oh! The joy. This great Pacific Ocean which we have been so long anxious to see, and the roaring noise made by waves breaking on rocky shores may be heard distinctly. [Clark]

Complete the chart by identifying which author wrote about each of the topics.

	Lewis	Clark	Other
1. description of hail storm		X	
2. friendly relations with Indians			
3. encounter with grizzly bear			
4. misunderstanding with Indians			
5. sighting of Pacific Ocean			
6. hiring of Charbonneau and Sacagawea			
7. camping at Hungry Creek			

EXPAND YOUR VOCABULARY

Decide whether the pairs of words are synonyms or antonyms. If they are synonyms, circle **S.** *If they are antonyms, circle* **A.**

1. purchase	sell	S	A
2. small	huge	S	A
3. chose	picked	S	A
4. expedition	journey	S	A
5. cordiality	hostility	S	A
6. hardships	difficulties	S	A
7. pursued	followed	S	A
8. plunged	jumped	S	A
9. joy	gladness	S	A

READING 2   How Factories Changed the United States

While the West was being explored, the Northeast was becoming industrialized. Before factories were built, workers made their products by hand, usually in their homes. The invention of new machines, however, led to the development of factories. People began leaving their homes on farms to move to cities and work in factories. They thought that factory work would be more interesting and that they would make more money. In truth, factory work was boring, dirty, dangerous, and unhealthy. In this article, you will read about the history of textile mills in New England.

BEFORE YOU READ

Look at the picture and read the caption. Describe what is going on in the picture. What do you think working conditions were like in the mid-1800s?

Women and children working in a textile factory in the 1800s

How Factories Changed the United States

1   From the early 1600s to the early 1800s, work in America was mostly centered around the home. Most people worked on farms, where they also made many needed goods—cloth, candles, tools, and furniture. Even specialized manufacturing, which blossomed during the 1700s, was home-centered. Skilled craftspeople made shoes, clothes, pots, and other goods in workshops attached to their homes.

2   As the demand for high-quality goods increased, many workshop owners hired helpers to work by their side. Though there were occasional disputes, the owners and their employees shared common interests. They usually understood each others' viewpoints.

3   An event occurred in 1790 that changed this personal relationship and led to decades of bitter labor conflict. The event was the construction of a water-powered textile mill at Pawtucket, Rhode Island, by an English mechanic named Sam Slater. Slater's powered machines were soon turning out huge quantities of high-quality cloth.

4   The demand for cloth soared and so did the number of textile mills in New England. In the 1820s, a group of businessmen built an entire factory town near the junction of the Connecticut and Merrimack Rivers in Massachusetts. The first mills were built there in 1822, and the town was named Lowell after the leading investor.

THE "LOWELL GIRLS"

5   In order to attract young women (mostly farmers' daughters) to the Lowell mills, schools, churches, social halls, and decent living quarters were built. The young women were encouraged to attend church and lectures and to save most of their earnings.

6   For a time, Lowell was viewed as a shining example of capitalism. However, competition from other mills and cheap imports from England forced the Lowell mill owners to cut costs. The managers increased the number of machines each woman had to operate, overcrowded the living quarters, and cut many social functions. The last straw for the workers was a wage cut in 1836. In protest, 1,500 mill workers went on strike.

7   But the strike failed. The mill owners were able to replace the "Yankee farm girls" with immigrants from Europe, who were eager to work at almost any wage. Factories rapidly became larger and competition stronger. As a result, factory owners tried hard to cut labor costs and increase output. Craft workers began to feel this pressure, too. In some cases, new machine tools replaced the need for craftsmen and their special skills.

CHANGING RELATIONSHIPS

8   The rise of the factory system changed employer-employee relations forever. Unlike the eighteenth-century workshop owner, the nineteenth-century factory owner had little contact with his employees. He was often less concerned with their well-being than with their cost.

9   Since more workers were usually available than jobs, protests over wages and working conditions rarely changed anything. Many workers realized that their only hope lay in collective action—union organization and the threat of strikes.

- info about general situation
- everything was made by hand
- shared common interests

- change the personal relationship

— Homework —

BUILD YOUR READING SKILLS: Recognizing Main Ideas

Check (✓) the topics that are discussed in Reading 2.

✓ **1.** what caused the change in the relationship between owners and workers

✓ **2.** why the number of textile mills in New England increased

✓ **3.** why Lowell mill owners were forced to cut costs

_____ **4.** problems of the farmers in the 1600s

✓ **5.** why Lowell mill workers went on strike

_____ **6.** the differences between eighteenth-century and nineteenth-century factory owners

_____ **7.** how much the factory paid the Lowell girls

CHECK YOUR COMPREHENSION

Circle the letter of the choice that best completes each sentence.

1. Until the early 1800s, most people worked _____.
   a. in factories
   b. at home
   c. in textile mills
   d. in big cities

2. Sam Slater _____.
   a. constructed a water-powered textile mill
   b. invented textiles
   c. started the Lowell factory
   d. organized unions

3. To cut costs, the Lowell mill owners _____.
   a. increased the number of machines each woman operated
   b. overcrowded the living quarters
   c. cut wages
   d. all of the above

4. The Lowell strike failed because _____.
   a. the owners gave the workers more money
   b. new machine tools were invented
   c. the owners were able to replace the girls with immigrants
   d. employee-employer relations improved

5. Many factory workers realized that they needed _____ to solve their problems.
   a. more social functions
   b. union organization
   c. new machine tools
   d. more pressure

EXPAND YOUR VOCABULARY

Circle the letter of the word that is closest in meaning to the word in bold type.

1. The **demand** for small cars is increasing.
   a. desire   **b.** price   **c.** fight

2. The price of oil **soared** in the 1980s.
   a. fell   **b.** stayed the same   **c.** rose

3. I had to clean the **entire** house before the party.
   a. whole   **b.** new   **c.** dirty

4. There are frequent **disputes** among the workers.
   a. discussions   **b.** arguments   **c.** agreements

5. We are excited about the **construction** of our new house.
   a. payment   **b.** color   **c.** building

6. If you want to save money, you need to **cut** costs.
   a. reduce   **b.** give up   **c.** trust

7. The town grew **rapidly** after the factory opened.
   a. slowly   **b.** quickly   **c.** evenly

8. The two brothers had a **conflict** over who would run the factory.
   a. disagreement   **b.** prize   **c.** contest

9. Mr. Lowell was the biggest **investor** in the mill.
   a. worker   **b.** troublemaker   **c.** financier

BUILD YOUR READING SKILLS: Understanding Transitions

Words and phrases that show the relationship between ideas, sentences, and paragraphs are called transitions. Recognizing transitions and understanding their meanings will help you become a more efficient reader. Look at the chart on page 36.

—HW—

TRANSITIONS

Time: Used to show the order in which events happen

first	at that time	later	subsequently
second	at the same time	meanwhile	then
third	before	next	today
after	during	now	when
as	finally	since	whenever
as soon as	from the start	soon	while
at present	from . . . to . . .		

Addition: Used to add another idea

also	besides	furthermore	moreover
and	finally	in addition	next
another	first	in addition to	second

Cause and effect: Used to express the cause or effect (result) of something

as	because	for	therefore
as a result	because of	since	thus
as a result of	consequently	so	

Comparison: Used to show similarities between things

as	just as	likewise	similarly
as well	like		

Contrast: Used to show differences between things

but	instead of	still	while
however	on the other hand	unlike	yet
in contrast	rather than	whereas	

Condition: Used to tell what must happen for something else to take place

if	otherwise	provided that	unless

Concession: Used to describe an unexpected result

although	even though	in spite of	still
despite	however	nevertheless	though
even if			

Illustration: Used to give examples

for example	including	like	such as
for instance			

Purpose: Used to show intent

for	in order to	so that

Read these sentences taken from Reading 2 and underline the transitions. Write the transition word(s) on the line and identify the type of relationship (for example, time, comparison, or illustration) it signifies. Refer to the chart on page 36.

1. From the early 1600s to the early 1800s, work in America was mostly centered around the home.

   Transition: _____   Type of relationship: _____

2. Though there were occasional disputes, the owners and their employees shared common interests.

   Transition: _____   Type of relationship: _____

3. Unlike the eighteenth-century workshop owner, the nineteenth-century factory owner had little contact with his employees.

   Transition: _____   Type of relationship: _____

4. Factories rapidly became larger and competition more fierce. As a result, factory owners tried hard to cut labor costs and increase output.

   Transition: _____   Type of relationship: _____

5. In order to attract young women (mostly farmers' daughters) to the Lowell mills, schools, churches, social halls, and decent living quarters were built.

   Transition: _____   Type of relationship: _____

6. Since more workers than jobs were usually available, protests over wages and working conditions rarely changed anything.

   Transition: _____   Type of relationship: _____

TALK ABOUT IT

Is the economy of your country based more on agriculture or industry? What do you think are the positive and negative effects of industrialization?

WRITE ABOUT IT

Pretend you are a worker at the Lowell mills in 1836. On a separate piece of paper, write a letter to a friend describing your life and the problems you are having with the owners.

-HW-

BUILD YOUR READING SKILLS: Understanding Dashes

Punctuation marks, such as dashes, often provide a clue to the meaning of an unfamiliar word or idea. Sometimes a dash means *that is* or *for example*.

A. *Look at the sentences that use dashes from Reading 2 on page 33 and answer the questions.*

1. Most people worked on farms, where they also made many needed goods—cloth, candles, tools, and furniture.

   What examples of "needed goods" does the author give?

   _____

2. Many workers realized that their only hope lay in collective action—union organization and the threat of strikes.

   What does the author mean by "collective action"?

   _____

B. *Read the passage "The Trail of Tears" on page 39. Use the dashes to help you answer these questions.*

1. What examples of Native American tribes does the author mention?

   _____

   _____

2. What types of hardships did the Cherokee have to face on their journey?

   _____

   _____

3. What lofty ideals does the author mention?

   _____

   _____

4. What did the Cherokee call their long march?

   _____

The Trail of Tears

1 The Cherokees were one of the largest and most important Native American tribes in the United States at the beginning of the eighteenth century. For hundreds of years, they had lived and farmed on land in northern Georgia. Then, in 1830, Congress passed the Indian Removal Act, which gave the U.S. government the right to relocate several Native American tribes—the Cherokees, Choctaws, Chickasaws, Creeks, and Seminoles—and give their land to white people. In 1838, President Andrew Jackson ordered the Cherokees to move off their homelands. He wanted to give their land to white settlers because gold had been discovered on it. Jackson sent military troops to gather Cherokee men, women, and children from Georgia and move them to Oklahoma. Although it was a bitterly cold winter, the Cherokees were forced to march over 1,200 miles. More than 4,000 Cherokees died from hardships—hunger, exposure, and disease. It is unfortunate that so many were treated so badly in a country founded on lofty ideals—that all people are created equal and have the right to life, liberty, and the pursuit of happiness. This sad time in history is now called the Trail of Tears—a translation from the Cherokee for the "Trail Where They Cried."

Native Americans were forced to move off their lands in the Trail of Tears.

While adventurers were exploring the West and northeasterners were building factories, southerners were turning to cotton production. Cotton could be cleaned much more quickly after the invention of the cotton gin. This helped farmers increase the amount of cotton they grew. However, as more cotton was produced, more slaves were needed.

AS YOU READ

As you read the article, underline the ways that the invention of the cotton gin changed the economy and society of the South.

Cotton Is King

1   In 1820, plantations in the South produced about 500,000 bales of cotton. By 1860, cotton production had jumped to nearly 5 million bales per year. For better or worse, King Cotton had taken over the southern economy.

2   Why did southern farmers plant so much more cotton than rice or tobacco? One reason was the cotton gin, invented by Eli Whitney in 1793. With this labor-saving device, seeds could be removed from the cotton plant fifty times faster than before. This made cotton a much more profitable crop.

3   Cotton was also a perfect export item because British clothing mills needed as much of it as they could get. At the start of the Civil War in 1861, cotton sales accounted for two-thirds of the nation's exports.

4   Beyond economics, the growth of the cotton industry affected southern culture and society as well. Because slaves performed nearly all the work on the plantations, the explosion of the cotton industry dramatically increased the need for slaves. The cotton gin changed the face of the South. After its

Cotton production took over the economy in the South.

invention, cotton plantations and slavery spread from the Carolinas to Louisiana. As cotton planting spread, the number of slaves continued to grow rapidly. After the turn of the century, the slave population of the United States more than tripled, from about 1.2 million in 1810 to almost 4 million in 1860.

CHECK YOUR COMPREHENSION

Answer the questions in complete sentences.

1. Why did southern farmers plant more cotton than any other crop?

   _____

   _____

   _____

   _____

2. Why was cotton a perfect export item?

   _____

   _____

   _____

   _____

3. Why did the explosion of the cotton industry increase the need for slaves?

   _____

   _____

   _____

   _____

CULTURE KERNEL

Congress rejected the adoption of the metric system in 1790 and again in 1821. The adoption continues to be rejected.

EXPAND YOUR VOCABULARY

Circle the letter of the choice that best completes each sentence.

1. The phonograph was _____ by Thomas Edison.

   a. profited   **b.** exported   **c.** invented

2. The phonograph is a _____ that plays recorded sounds.

   a. device   **b.** plantation   **c.** reason

3. Wheat is an important _____ crop for Canada.

   a. culture   **b.** export   **c.** device

4. The population of the United States _____ with the arrival of new immigrants.

   a. invented   **b.** decreased   **c.** swelled

5. Cotton was grown on _____ in the South.

   a. devices   **b.** plantations   **c.** slaves

BUILD YOUR READING SKILLS: Scanning

Scan Reading 3 to complete the exercise.

_____ **1.** the number of bales of cotton the South produced in 1820

_____ **2.** the person who invented the cotton gin

_____ **3.** when the Civil War started

_____ **4.** the number of slaves in the United States in 1810

_____ **5.** the year the cotton gin was invented

_____ **6.** the number of bales of cotton the South produced in 1860

_____ **7.** the number of slaves in the United States in 1860

a. 1793

b. 1.2 million

c. almost 4 million

d. 5 million

e. 500,000

f. Eli Whitney

g. 1861

LINKING PAST TO PRESENT With the invention of the cotton gin in 1793, cotton could be cleaned much more quickly after it was picked. Like many other labor- and time-saving inventions, the cotton gin was the result of creative thinking and the desire for efficiency. Americans still look for easier, quicker, and cheaper ways of doing things.

REACT AND RESPOND What present-day examples can you think of that illustrate the desire of Americans to do things easily, quickly, and cheaply? Do you think that doing things quickly and cheaply is usually the best way? Why or why not?

TALK ABOUT IT

What do you think are some of the most important inventions in history? Choose five and write them in order of importance.

1. _____

2. _____

3. _____

4. _____

5. _____

WRITE ABOUT IT

What invention do you think has had the most important impact on our lives?
You may choose one from the list or one of your own. On a separate piece of
paper, write a paragraph defending your choice.

1. printing press
2. airplane
3. penicillin
4. steam engine
5. microscope
6. computer

READING 4 Transcendentalism: A New View

A philosophy called transcendentalism became influential in the
United States during the 1830s. Transcendentalists were idealistic and
optimistic. They were a force for social reform. The transcendentalists
strongly influenced both the antislavery and women's rights
movements. They also helped improve conditions for workers and
education for all children. The spirit of individualism that was so
important in the growth of the United States can be seen in many of
their beliefs and actions. In this article, you will read about the
development of transcendentalism in the United States.

AS YOU READ

Read the first two paragraphs of the article and discuss what you see when you
look at a tree.

Transcendentalism: A New View
by D. H. DeFord and H. S. Stout

When you look at a tree, what do you see?

1   When you look at a tree, what do you
see? A great chance to climb? Shade for a
picnic lunch?

2   Imagine a group of people standing
around the tree. One man is a carpenter.
He looks at the tree and thinks of the
lumber it could provide to build a house.
The woman standing next to him works in
a paper factory. She sees the tree as raw
material for paper pulp. Another person
imagines a home for birds and squirrels
and insects, and someone else thinks of a
beautiful piece of furniture.

(continues on next page)

3   Different people often see things differently. What they see and how they understand it depends on their point of view.

4   In the early 1800s, most people in New England believed that the only way to know anything was through the physical senses—sight, hearing, touch, taste, and smell. They also said that to understand the "facts" gained through the senses, a person must think logically about those facts. This was their point of view.

5   A few people disagreed. These people became known as the transcendentalists. (The word *transcend* means "to go beyond." *Transcendental* means "to go beyond the five senses.") They believed that the closer to nature people stayed, the better they would be. They thought that people have a sense, which some called intuition, that is not physical. Using intuition, people can know what is "true and right and beautiful" without logical thinking. According to transcendentalism, people could lose their sense of intuition if they lost touch with nature. For example, think about the tree we considered earlier. The group of people around it might say, "Our town is growing and changing. That tree should be cut down and used to make a house." That point of view would make sense of chopping down the tree. But maybe you believe the tree needs to stand as a home for the animals. In that case, you might feel the town is changing and growing in the wrong way.

6   The transcendentalists had this sort of problem. They saw the United States growing and changing quickly. Although many people thought the growth and changes were good, the transcendentalists did not. They saw slavery advancing, American Indians being massacred, and forests being cut down. They felt that these changes grew out of a wrong point of view.

7   The transcendentalists believed that the country would change for the better only when individuals improved. For that to happen, they thought, people needed to simplify their lives. Only then would they return to the natural intuition with which they were born and which would show them what was true, right, and beautiful.

8   To encourage their point of view, transcendentalist leaders met as a group. They met to talk about new ways to see and understand the world and themselves. They considered philosophers from ancient Greece, the Orient, and Germany, and they reconsidered the religion of the Puritans. But they did much more than talk.

9   Most transcendentalists supported social reform movements, including equal rights for women and temperance (abstinence from alcohol) and those opposing war and slavery. One of the more famous transcendentalists was Ralph Waldo Emerson. As a writer, minister, and lecturer, he became an important spokesman for transcendentalism. He also inspired a group of American writers that included Henry David Thoreau, Walt Whitman, Nathaniel Hawthorne, and Emily Dickinson.

10   A number of transcendentalists started experimental communities, such as Brook Farm and Fruitlands in Massachusetts. These communities were intended to be utopias, or perfect societies. For instance, you might start a utopian community if you were as concerned about all trees as you were about the one we looked at earlier. In your utopia, trees would be saved for wildlife. In the same way, the

transcendentalists hoped to correct what they thought were wrong choices in the changing United States, at least in their own small communities. None of these communities lasted long, however.

11   Once the Civil War began, the transcendental movement began to die out with the passing of its foremost leaders. But the point of view they held has not died. It lives on in the continuing American dream of a perfect society. It lives on, too, in some Americans' interest in Eastern philosophy and religion and in the conservation of nature. And it lives on in the literature of Ralph Waldo Emerson and the writers he inspired. Their work grew directly out of the transcendental movement, and it continues to be read and loved today.

BUILD YOUR TEST-TAKING SKILLS

Circle the letter of the choice that best completes each sentence.

1. Many transcendentalists took part in _____.
   a. social reform movements
   b. experimental communities
   c. philosophical discussions
   d. all of the above

2. The term *transcendental* describes _____.
   a. facts gained through the senses
   b. the way people see things
   c. knowledge transcending the five senses
   d. none of the above

3. The transcendentalists supported all of the following except _____.
   a. the massacre of Native Americans
   b. abstinence from alcohol
   c. equal rights for women
   d. the conservation of nature

4. The transcendental movement began to die out by _____.
   a. the Civil War
   b. the beginning of the nineteenth century
   c. 1833
   d. the early 1800s

5. Transcendentalists believed that intuition _____.
   a. was one of the physical senses
   b. was a logical way of thinking
   c. was a way to know something without logical thinking
   d. had nothing to do with nature

CHECK YOUR COMPREHENSION

Check (✓) the statements that transcendentalists would agree with.

_____ 1. People are born knowing what is good, even before they know the words to describe goodness.

_____ 2. The only way to know anything is through the physical senses.

_____ 3. The closer to nature people stay, they better they will be.

_____ 4. The growth and changes occurring in the United States in the early 1800s were good.

_____ 5. In order to understand "facts" gained through the senses, a person must think logically about those facts.

_____ 6. The United States can change for the better only when individuals improve.

_____ 7. Women deserve equal rights.

_____ 8. Forests should not be cut down.

_____ 9. Slavery is necessary for the economy.

EXPAND YOUR VOCABULARY

A. *Match each word or expression from the reading with its meaning.*

_____ 1. logical   **a.** perfect society

_____ 2. massacred   **b.** agree with

_____ 3. reform   **c.** disappear

_____ 4. utopia   **d.** go beyond

_____ 5. die out   **e.** improve

_____ 6. support   **f.** killed

_____ 7. transcend   **g.** reasonable

_____ 8. intuition   **h.** knowledge without logical thinking

B. *Mark each item true (**T**) or false (**F**).*

_____ 1. When you support a movement, you are against it.

_____ 2. When the transcendental movement died out, it increased in size.

_____ 3. If you use your intuition, you use your feelings.

_____ 4. If you support something, you don't want it to happen.

_____ 5. Brook Farm was supposed to be a utopia since the founders wanted it to be a perfect community.

_____ 6. When the Native Americans were massacred, they were killed.

_____ **7.** People who take part in reform movements want to change something about society.

_____ **8.** If something is logical, it makes sense.

LINKING PAST TO PRESENT The transcendentalists influenced social reform movements, such as the antislavery and women's rights movements of their time. Later, their writings on nonviolence inspired modern leaders such as Mohandas Gandhi and Martin Luther King Jr. In many ways, the transcendentalists were typical of the spirit of individualism that has fueled growth and change in the United States.

REACT AND RESPOND In general, how do you think Americans are independent in their thinking? Can you think of anyone in your country or the United States who is working today to solve social problems?

HISTORY MAKER: Henry David Thoreau

Carefully read the list of facts about transcendentalist Henry David Thoreau. Then choose the information you want from the list to write a paragraph about him on a separate piece of paper. Be sure to begin your paragraph with a topic sentence that states the main idea. Include transition words to guide the reader from one point to the next.

- was a writer, philosopher, naturalist
- born in 1817 and died in 1862 in Concord, Massachusetts
- was quiet, introverted, liked the world of ideas
- graduated from Harvard College in 1837
- withdrew from society for two years to live alone in a one-room cabin he built himself (for $28) near Walden Pond in Concord, Massachusetts
- spent his days at Walden Pond observing and writing about nature
- wrote *Walden,* a book about his life at Walden Pond
- believed people should not obey laws they don't agree with
- against slavery
- refused to pay taxes for six years to protest that government allowed slavery
- arrested in 1846 because he refused to pay taxes
- his beliefs in peaceful resistance influenced Mohandas Gandhi and Martin Luther King Jr.

Exchange your paragraph with a partner. Read your partner's paragraph and check it for correct grammar, punctuation, and capitalization.

SKILL REVIEW: Understanding Transitions

With industrialization, it became necessary to transport manufactured goods from factories to consumers. In the early 1800s, many canals and roads were built to improve transportation. The canals joined rivers to the Great Lakes and made it cheaper and easier to move goods and people.

Read the passage about the building of the Erie Canal and underline the transitions. Then, complete the exercise that follows by writing the transition words on the lines provided and identifying the type of relationship they signify. Refer to the chart on page 36.

Horses pull a boat along a canal.

The Erie Canal

1   The forty-foot-wide and four-foot-deep Erie Canal was the greatest engineering wonder of its day. When the canal linking the Great Lakes to the Hudson River was finished, it changed the country in ways even more dramatic than New York's governor DeWitt Clinton had promised.

2   Freight rates fell by 90 percent. In addition, travel times along the canal dropped substantially. For instance, the canal cut the twenty-day trip between Albany and Buffalo to just eight days.

3   Meanwhile, towns along the canal, such as Rochester and Syracuse, boomed. Settlers and their belongings crowded Clinton's Ditch, as the canal

was called, on their way to the new states of the Northwest Territory. After the canal opened in 1825, the number of settlers bound for Michigan, Ohio, Indiana, and Illinois increased tenfold.

4   The canal also made it easier for western settlers to ship their produce back to markets in the East. New York City benefited most from this huge increase in trade. New York profited again when manufactured goods from all over the Northeast passed through the city on their way to the canal and the interior of the country. Soon, news of huge profits from the Erie Canal convinced other states to build canals linking the nation's major waterways.

1. Transition: _____   Type of relationship: _____

2. Transition: _____   Type of relationship: _____

3. Transition: _____   Type of relationship: _____

4. Transition: _____   Type of relationship: _____

5. Transition: _____   Type of relationship: _____

6. Transition: _____   Type of relationship: _____

7. Transition: _____   Type of relationship: _____

8. Transition: _____   Type of relationship: _____

9. Transition: _____   Type of relationship: _____

PUT IT TOGETHER

Discuss the questions.

1. Reformers in the early 1800s wanted to improve the treatment of prisoners and the mentally ill. In what ways do you think better treatment of prisoners and the mentally ill might improve society as a whole?

2. The people who explored the western territories of the United States in the early days faced many dangers and took many risks. They were adventurous. Do you consider yourself adventurous? Would you be interested in exploring unknown territories?

3. Who are the national heroes in your country? Why have these people become heroes? What qualities do they possess that your culture admires?

CHAPTER 3

A DIVIDED NATION

The Mid-1800s

*I*n this chapter, you will read about the California Gold Rush, the growth of cities, and the deepening divisions between the North and the South.

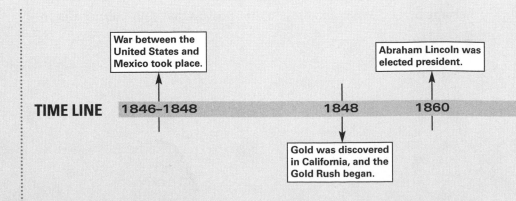

What was happening in your country in the mid-1800s?

TIME LINE

War between the United States and Mexico took place.

Abraham Lincoln was elected president.

1846–1848   1848   1860

Gold was discovered in California, and the Gold Rush began.

The United States in the Mid-1800s

Many of the trends that started in the early 1800s continued into the mid-1800s.

Expansion to the West Coast

The western frontier continued to attract many people. In 1848, gold was discovered in California. Approximately 90,000 people rushed to California hoping to get rich. In addition to Americans, many people from China, Latin America, Australia, and Europe came looking for gold. Very few miners found enough gold to get rich, but they helped settle and develop the West. By the middle of the century, the borders of the United States stretched from the Atlantic to the Pacific Oceans.

Growth of Cities

During this period, cities grew more quickly than ever before. Factories were built in and near cities. People poured into the cities from the countryside and from abroad. Over 2 million more immigrants came to the United States during the 1840s and 1850s. They saw the United States as a land of opportunity where anything was possible. As cities grew in size, serious problems developed. Life in the cities, especially for immigrants, was difficult. They faced poverty, pollution, and overcrowding.

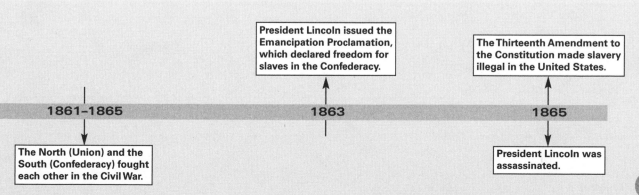

President Lincoln issued the Emancipation Proclamation, which declared freedom for slaves in the Confederacy.

The Thirteenth Amendment to the Constitution made slavery illegal in the United States.

1861–1865 **1863** **1865**

The North (Union) and the South (Confederacy) fought each other in the Civil War.

President Lincoln was assassinated.

The Civil War

While the country's borders moved westward, the differences between the North and South became deeper. The biggest difference involved the issue of slavery. During the 1840s and 1850s, the southern economy became more dependent on slavery. At the same time, many northerners continued to oppose slavery. As the antislavery, or abolitionist, movement got stronger, tensions between the North and South increased. Slavery was an emotional issue because it threatened two important American beliefs: individual freedom and democratic principles. In 1860, Abraham Lincoln was elected president. He believed the United States could not continue half slave and half free. After Lincoln became president, eleven southern slave states separated from the United States and formed their own government, called the Confederate States of America. In 1861, civil war between the North (Union) and the South (Confederacy) broke out. The Civil War almost destroyed the United States, but it also brought freedom to 4 million slaves.

After four years of bloody fighting, the South surrendered on April 9, 1865, and the country was united once again. Within eight months, Congress passed the Thirteenth Amendment to the Constitution, abolishing slavery in the United States.

Answer the questions.

1. What trends continued from the beginning of the century?

    a. _____

    b. _____

    c. _____

2. What problems did people who lived in cities face?

    a. _____

    b. _____

    c. _____

3. What are two things that Abraham Lincoln believed in?

    a. _____

    b. _____

4. What two groups fought each other in the Civil War?

    a. _____

    b. _____

This article tells the story of a man named Levi Strauss. He went to California during the Gold Rush, but it was not his plan to get rich by finding gold. His plan was to get rich by selling material for tents and wagon covers to the miners. As you will find out, he changed his plans to fit the needs of the miners and created one of the world's most successful companies.

BEFORE YOU READ

Discuss these questions with your classmates.

1. How many people in your classroom are wearing blue jeans right now?

2. What are some of the most popular brands of blue jeans in your country? Is Levi's a popular brand?

3. What are some places where it is appropriate to wear jeans in your country? Are there some places where you wouldn't wear jeans? For example, would you wear jeans to work, school, a nice restaurant, a nightclub, or church?

Now read the article one time quickly and look for the main idea.

Levi's Gold
by Dorothy Slate

1   When the clipper ship sailed through California's Golden Gate that March day in 1853, twenty-four-year-old Levi Strauss rushed to the deck, eager to see San Francisco. The Gold Rush, started in 1848, still attracted men by the thousands to seek their fortunes. Strauss was one of them.

2   Six years earlier, he had left Bavaria in Germany to escape unfair laws against Jews and to join his older brothers, Jonas and Louis, in New York. They taught him English and told him peddling was an honorable occupation in the United States. Now he faced a new challenge. In his baggage were goods to sell. His brothers had helped select them in New York before he left on his long voyage around Cape Horn to California. Gold miners were sure to need thread, needles, scissors, thimbles, and rolls of canvas cloth for tents and wagon covers.

3   As Strauss looked toward the city, he saw several small boats approaching the ship. When they came close, some of their passengers asked for news from the East. Others climbed aboard to see what merchandise the ship had brought. In a short while, Strauss had sold almost everything he had brought with him. Only the rolls of canvas remained.

4   Stepping ashore, he saw a busy city with many "stores" that were merely tents

(continues on next page)

A miner pans for gold in California.

or shacks. Among the ironworks, billiard-table manufacturers, dry-goods stores, breweries, and hundreds of saloons stood some stranded ships serving as hotels.

5   With gold dust from his sales aboard ship, Strauss bought a cart. He loaded his rolls of canvas and pushed the cart along wood-planked sidewalks. He parked on Montgomery Street, waiting for miners to pass by.

6   A miner stopped to look at his canvas.

7   "It's for tenting," Strauss explained.

8   "You should have brought pants," the prospector told him. "Pants don't wear well in the mines. Can't get a pair strong enough to last."

9   Instantly, the young entrepreneur found a tailor and created the first pair of jeans. The demand for "Levi's" grew so fast that Strauss could hardly keep up with it. When the brown canvas was gone, he switched to a sturdy fabric, *serge de Nimes*, from Nimes, France. The name was

quickly shortened to "denim," and Strauss adopted the indigo blue cloth familiar today.

10   Levi's brothers, Jonas and Louis, were his partners, as was David Stern, who had married Levi's sister, Fanny. They decided to call their firm Levi Strauss & Company, agreeing that Levi was the "business head" in the family. Years went by, and the business grew.

11   Then, in July 1872, a letter arrived from Jacob W. Davis, a tailor in Reno, Nevada. The letter explained that he was now reinforcing pants pocket corners with copper rivets. Rivets strengthened the seams, which tore out when miners and other workers stuffed their pockets with gold nuggets and tools.

12   Davis got so many orders that he worried someone would steal his idea. If Levi Strauss & Company would take out a patent in his name, Davis would give them half the right to sell the riveted clothing.

13   Strauss immediately saw the profit potential. Instead of nine or ten dollars a dozen, the riveted pants could bring thirty-six dollars—just for adding a penny's worth of metal. It was a good risk.

14   The U.S. Patent Office took its time in granting Strauss a patent. It took ten months and many revisions and amendments before the Patent Office agreed that the idea of riveted pockets was unusual enough to be patented.

15   When Davis moved his family to San Francisco, Strauss put him in charge of production. Soon a force of sixty women stitched Levi's on a piecework basis. The orange thread still used today was an attempt to match the copper rivets. Another still-used trademark is the leather label featuring two men whipping a pair of horses trying to tear apart the riveted pants.

16   Successful in business, Levi Strauss still found time to participate in many civic organizations and was well liked in San Francisco's business community. He never married, saying, "I am a bachelor, and I fancy on that account I need to work more, for my entire life is my business."

17   Although he had no children of his own, Strauss established many scholarships at the University of California, and when he died in 1902, he left money to Protestant, Catholic, and Jewish (orphanages.) He left the business to his sister Fanny's children.

18   Levi Strauss found gold not in streams or mines, but in fulfilling an everyday need. Today, presidents, movie stars, and millions of other people wear Levi's and other brands of denim jeans, clothing created by an entrepreneur who responded to the needs of the market.

BUILD YOUR READING SKILLS: Recognizing Main Ideas

Circle the number of the statement that best expresses the main idea of Reading 1.

1. Gold miners bought Levi's pants because they were strong and durable.

2. Levi Strauss was able to make his fortune in jeans by responding to the needs of the market.

3. Levi was the "business head" of the Strauss family.

4. Levi Strauss was successful in business, but he still found time to participate in civic organizations.

CULTURE KERNEL

American football began in the mid-1800s as a combination of rugby and soccer. Football is still one of the most popular sports in the United States.

Now reread the article more carefully and do the exercises that follow.

CHECK YOUR COMPREHENSION

A. *Mark each item true (T) or false (F).*

___F___ 1. Levi Strauss made his fortune from digging for gold.

___T___ 2. Levi's pants became popular very quickly.

___T___ 3. Gold miners bought Levi's pants because they were strong and durable.

___F___ 4. Levi brought canvas cloth to San Francisco to make pants for the gold miners.

___F___ 5. Levi thought of using copper rivets to reinforce pocket corners.

___T___ 6. Levi Strauss was able to make his fortune in jeans by responding to the needs of the market.

___T___ 7. Denim jeans are more popular today than they were in 1850.

B. *Circle the letter of the choice that best completes each sentence.*

1. When Strauss used up his supply of brown canvas he switched to a fabric called _____C_____.
   a. copper   c. denim
   b. tenting   d. gold

2. _____b_____ invented the idea of using copper rivets to reinforce pocket corners.
   a. Jonas Strauss   c. David Stern
   b. Jacob W. Davis   d. Fanny Strauss

3. Levi Strauss established many _____a_____ at the University of California.
   a. scholarships   c. markets
   b. orphanages   d. patents

4. Today, Levi's jeans are still made with _____d_____.
   a. orange thread   c. leather labels
   b. riveted pockets   d. all of the above

5. _____C_____ Strauss was the "business head" of the family.
   a. Fanny   c. Levi
   b. Jonas   d. Louis

EXPAND YOUR VOCABULARY

A. *Complete each sentence with a word from the list.*

fortune   occupation   baggage   cloth   revisions

profit   entrepreneur   participate   bachelor   merchandise

1. My grandfather was an _____ who started his own business when he was still in his teens. When he retired, he had made a _____.

2. If you like working with people, you should consider an _____ in the field of education, medicine, or psychology.

3. I bought a used car for $2,000. After I fixed it up, I sold it for $3,500. I made a $1,500 _____ on the deal.

4. Cotton is used to make _____.

5. My uncle has never gotten married. He's still a _____.

6. The teacher asked the student to make some _____ in his essay.

7. I'm too shy to _____ in class discussions.

8. My _____ was light enough to carry onto the train myself.

9. What kind of _____ does that store sell?

B. *Match each word from the reading with its synonym.*

_C_ 1. revisions   **a.** fabric

_d_ 2. occupation   **b.** luggage

_a_ 3. cloth   **c.** changes

_e_ 4. merchandise   **d.** job

_b_ 5. baggage   **e.** goods

BUILD YOUR READING SKILLS: Understanding Sequencing

To understand the past, you need to recognize the sequence of events, *the order in which things happened. Reread Reading 1 and put the list of events in the correct time order by numbering them from 1 to 7.*

_3_ **a.** Levi sold his first pair of pants.

_2_ **b.** Levi left Germany to join his brothers in New York.

_6_ **c.** Davis devised a way to reinforce pocket corners with copper rivets.

_1_ **d.** The Gold Rush started.

_4_ **e.** Levi began using blue denim to make his pants.

_5_ **f.** Levi Strauss & Company was established.

_7_ **g.** Levi left his business to his sister's children.

Pioneers heading west traveled in covered wagons. By the 1860s, more than 300,000 people had traveled by these wagon trains. Then railroads took over, and migration was faster but no longer a great adventure.

Pioneers head west in a wagon train.

LINKING PAST TO PRESENT Self-made men, like Levi Strauss, have always been admired in the United States. Today, entrepreneurs continue to hold a highly respected place in American society.

REACT AND RESPOND What was the main reason that Levi Strauss was so successful? What other reasons can you think of that contributed to his success? What qualities does a person need in order to be a successful entrepreneur? Why do you think that entrepreneurs are respected in society?

WRITE ABOUT IT

Pretend that you work for the Levi Strauss & Company today. On a separate piece of paper, write a paragraph for the new employee handbook describing how the company got started.

| READING 2 | **Urbanization: The Growth of Cities** |

While the Gold Rush was going on in the West, cities in the Northeast were growing rapidly. At the end of the Revolutionary War in 1783, there were only 5 cities in North America with 8,000 or more people. By 1850, there were 141. The change was most noticeable in New York City, where new factories, railroads, and telegraph lines created ideal conditions for expansion. In this article, you will read about the causes and effects of urbanization.

Urbanization: The Growth of Cities

1 In the decade before the Civil War, U.S. cities grew three times faster than the rest of the country. One cause of this population shift was a decrease in the number of northeastern farmers. Many found it increasingly difficult to compete with low-priced crops being shipped in from the West.

2 Another cause was the increase in European immigration. Between 1840 and

1860, 4 million immigrants arrived in the United States, and most settled in the northern port cities where they landed. During this twenty-year period, the population of New York City rose from 312,000 to 813,000, and the output of goods from U.S. factories doubled.

3   The jobs that cities offered were an important attraction, but (urban) areas had problems as well. During the 1850s, most cities had no public transportation, and only rich people could afford carriages. As a result, poor people had to live within walking distance of the factories where they worked. This led to overcrowding, pollution, and (sanitation) problems.

4   Although larger cities began to build public water and sewage systems during the 1850s, most had no means of controlling pollution or even removing garbage. Hogs roamed over much of New York City, eating garbage littering the streets of poorer neighborhoods.

New York City in 1850

BUILD YOUR TEST-TAKING SKILLS

Circle the letter of the choice that best completes each sentence or answers the question.

1. The article mainly discusses _____.
   a. the growth of cities in the mid-1800s
   b. the pollution problem in cities
   c. the increase in immigration between 1840 and 1860
   d. the types of jobs available in cities

2. Which of the following is not mentioned as a problem in cities in the mid-1800s?
   a. overcrowding   c. jobs
   b. pollution   d. sanitation

3. The author describes the immigration trend in the middle of the nineteenth century in paragraph _____.
   a. 1   c. 3
   b. 2   d. 4

4. It can be concluded from the article that _____.
   a. northeastern farmers were making huge profits
   b. factory jobs in the cities were easy to get
   c. only rich people could afford to take public transportation
   d. most cities did not begin to control pollution until the 1860s

5. The word *decade* in paragraph 1 is closest in meaning to _____.
   a. a ten-year period
   b. a twenty-year period
   c. a century
   d. months

6. The word *most* in the first sentence of paragraph 4 refers to _____.
   a. sewage systems
   b. hogs
   c. public water
   d. larger cities

7. The word *shift* in paragraph 1 is closest in meaning to _____.
   a. increase
   b. decrease
   c. change
   d. status

 LINKING PAST TO PRESENT At the end of the Revolutionary War in 1783, there were five cities in the United States with 8,000 or more people. By the end of the twentieth century, there were more than 130 cities with populations of 100,000 to 250,000 or more.

REACT AND RESPOND Do you live in an urban, suburban, or rural area? Do you like living where you are, or would you rather live in one of the other types of areas? What are the advantages and disadvantages of living in each type of area?

READING 3   The Underground Railroad

While the country was moving west, the divisions between the North and South worsened. The issue of slavery divided the country. Some antislavery northerners, mostly blacks, helped runaway slaves escape to free states or to Canada. The journey to freedom was difficult for these runaway slaves. They traveled only at night and had to find places to hide during the day. In this article, you will read about a secret organization of people that helped runaway slaves reach safety in the North.

BEFORE YOU READ

Study the map of the United States in 1861 that shows how the nation was divided. Use the map to answer the questions.

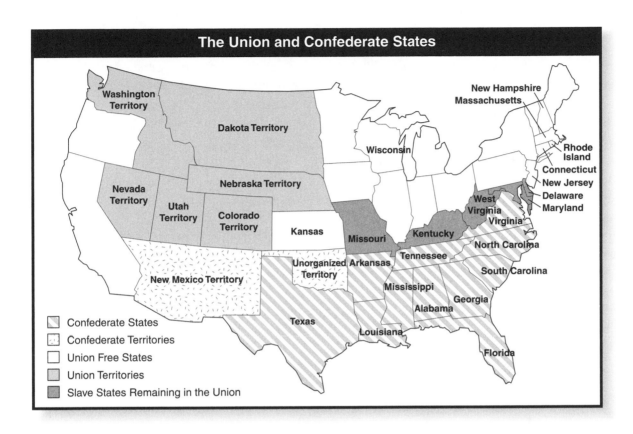

The Union and Confederate States

Washington Territory
Dakota Territory
New Hampshire
Massachusetts
Wisconsin
Rhode Island
Connecticut
New Jersey
Delaware
Maryland
Nevada Territory
Nebraska Territory
Utah Territory
Colorado Territory
West Virginia
Virginia
Kansas
Kentucky
Missouri
North Carolina
Unorganized Territory
Arkansas
Tennessee
New Mexico Territory
South Carolina
Mississippi
Georgia
Alabama
Texas
Louisiana
Florida

- Confederate States
- Confederate Territories
- Union Free States
- Union Territories
- Slave States Remaining in the Union

1. Which five slave states did not join the Confederacy?

   _____

2. How many states joined the Confederacy? _____

3. Did the states that bordered Wisconsin belong to the Confederacy or the Union? _____

4. How many Union territories were there? _____

The Underground Railroad

1 The Underground Railroad was neither underground nor a railroad. Instead, it was a system used before the Civil War to help runaway slaves reach freedom in the North and Canada.

2 Railway terms were often used to describe the way the Underground Railroad worked. The routes taken by runaway slaves were called lines. The safe houses at which they stopped were stations. The sympathetic whites and free blacks who risked their lives to lead slaves out of the South were conductors. The slaves were called packages or freight.

3 The most famous conductor on the Underground Railroad was Harriet Tubman. After escaping slavery in 1849, Tubman returned to the South on many occasions to help rescue others. She demonstrated her courage and commitment time and time again by personally leading more than 300 slaves to freedom. Tubman was called the "Moses of her people," after the biblical hero who led the Jews out of slavery in Egypt.

4 Notable among the whites who participated in the Underground Railroad was Harriet Beecher Stowe, the author of *Uncle Tom's Cabin*. Between 1832 and 1850, Stowe lived in Cincinnati, just across the Ohio River from the slave state of Kentucky. Stowe learned a great deal about plantation life from the slaves she helped to escape. Many of these stories later appeared in her book.

Slaves on the Underground Railroad

BUILD YOUR READING SKILLS: Recognizing Main Ideas

Write the number of the paragraph that . . .

_____ **a.** defines the terms that describe how the railroad worked.

_____ **b.** mentions the book *Uncle Tom's Cabin.*

_____ **c.** describes what the Underground Railroad was.

_____ **d.** talks about Harriet Tubman.

EXPAND YOUR VOCABULARY

Complete each sentence with a word from the list.

demonstrated   escaped   commitment

courage   notable

1. He _____ his ability to speak English by ordering our dinners in the restaurant.

2. Marriage is an important _____.

3. Many slaves _____ from the South on the Underground Railroad.

4. The conductors showed great _____ on the Underground Railroad.

5. There are many _____ people and events in our history.

BUILD YOUR READING SKILLS: Scanning

Scan Reading 3 to complete the exercise.

f **1.** conductors   **a.** routes taken by runaway slaves

g **2.** Harriet Beecher Stowe   **b.** safe houses where runaway slaves stopped

e **3.** 1849   **c.** "Moses of her people"

a **4.** lines   **d.** runaway slaves

c **5.** Harriet Tubman   **e.** year Harriet Tubman escaped slavery

b **6.** stations   **f.** people who helped slaves out of South

d **7.** freight   **g.** author of *Uncle Tom's Cabin*

BUILD YOUR DICTIONARY SKILLS

One of the most important reasons for using a dictionary is to learn the meaning of a word. Since many words in English have more than one meaning, the dictionary lists all of the meanings.

The dictionary also tells you the part of speech of each word. The parts of speech are abbreviated as follows: n. = noun; v. = verb; adj. = adjective; adv. = adverb. In English, some words have the same form for both the noun and the verb. These words change their meaning when they are used as different parts of speech. For example: *That movie was a big* hit. *I* hit *the ball with the bat.* In the first sentence, *hit* is a noun. In the second sentence, *hit* is a verb.

Use a dictionary to determine the part of speech of the word in bold type in each sentence. Then write the correct definition.

1. Railway **terms** were often used to describe the way the Underground Railroad worked. (_____)

   _____

2. You will have three exams during the **term**. (_____)

   _____

3. He is someone I would **term** "irresponsible." (_____)

   _____

4. The safe houses at which they **stopped** were stations. (_____)

   _____

5. Meet me at the bus **stop**. (_____)

   _____

6. I have to make two **stops** on the way to work—one at the library and the other at the dry cleaners. (_____)

   _____

7. The sympathetic whites and free blacks who **risked** their lives to lead slaves out of the South were conductors. (_____)

   _____

8. When you invest in stocks, you take a **risk** with your money. (_____)

   _____

CULTURE KERNEL

The invention of the camera in 1839 allowed people to photograph the horrors of war. This was the first time in U.S. history that people could see true-to-life pictures from battles.

9. Stowe learned a great **deal** about plantation life from the slaves she helped to escape. (_____)

_____

10. To begin, **deal** each player six cards. (_____)

_____

Clara Barton: "The Angel of the Battlefield"

The Civil War (1861–1865) was one of the saddest periods in American history. The war was long and bloody, and it split the country. More than 600,000 men died, and more than 1,100,000 were injured. Civil War soldiers entered the army at a time when weapons had just become more powerful and more deadly. In addition, during the mid-1800s people knew very little about the causes and cures of diseases or how to prevent them from spreading. Also, little was known about sanitation and nutrition. Doctors rarely used antiseptics and operated in the field in very unsanitary conditions. In this article, you will learn about a courageous woman who nursed wounded men on the battlefields.

Civil War surgery

Clara Barton:
"The Angel of the Battlefield"
by James Ciment

1   Clara Barton was born in Oxford, Massachusetts, the youngest of five children. At the age of fifteen, she became a teacher and soon afterward started a school in New Jersey. The school grew very quickly, but authorities didn't feel it was proper for a woman to run it, and she was forced to resign.

2   Then, in 1861, Barton received a new calling. After the first battles of the Civil War, she witnessed the terrible conditions the wounded were forced to endure. Infection and disease spread quickly throughout field surgeries and hospitals, as few surgeons sterilized their equipment, rooms were not kept clean, and the same bandages were used repeatedly. The wounded were feverish and dying from disease and infection. There were few nurses to ease their pain. Barton quickly organized a network of contributors to purchase food and supplies. She gained permission to pass through battle lines tending the wounded. Her post, she said, was "the open field between the bullet and the hospital." Through her hard work, the number of deaths from disease and infection greatly decreased.

3   As a military nurse, Barton came to realize the importance of providing aid to the wounded. It was she who founded the American Red Cross and who convinced more than a dozen countries to recognize the neutrality of the Red Cross flag.

4   Barton's humanitarian work did not stop after the Civil War ended. She became dedicated to helping the newly emancipated blacks find jobs and housing. She also began a national effort to find missing soldiers.

CHECK YOUR COMPREHENSION

A. *Mark each item true (**T**) or false (**F**).*

___F___ **1.** Clara Barton is best remembered for starting a school in New Jersey.

___I___ **2.** The spreading of infection and disease was a serious problem for Civil War soldiers.

___F___ **3.** There were many nurses helping the wounded during the Civil War.

___T___ **4.** Barton convinced many countries to accept the neutrality of the Red Cross flag.

___I___ **5.** Barton helped improve conditions for wounded soldiers.

B. *Circle the letter of the choice that best completes each sentence or answers the question.*

1. Barton was forced to resign from her position as head of a school in New Jersey because _____.
   a. there were so few students
   b. it was too expensive to run a private school
   c. authorities didn't feel it was proper for a woman to run it
   d. the Civil War started

2. Infection and disease spread quickly because _____.
   a. few surgeons sterilized their equipment
   b. rooms were not kept clean
   c. the same bandages were used repeatedly
   d. all of the above

3. Barton helped decrease _____.
   a. the number of Civil War soldiers who died from disease and infection
   b. the number of battles fought in the war
   c. the amount of food and supplies given to the soldiers
   d. the amount of time soldiers spent fighting

4. Which of the following is not mentioned in the article as an accomplishment of Barton's?
   a. She provided aid to wounded soldiers in the Civil War.
   b. She started a school in New Jersey.
   c. She was one of the first women to graduate from medical school.
   d. She founded the American Red Cross.

EXPAND YOUR VOCABULARY

Circle the letter of the word that is closest in meaning to the word in bold type.

1. The school grew very quickly, but authorities didn't feel it was **proper** for a woman to run it, and she was forced to **resign**.

   proper
   a. appropriate   b. sad   c. clear

   resign
   a. join   b. pay   c. quit

2. After the first battles of the Civil War, she witnessed the terrible conditions the **wounded** were forced to endure.
   a. hurt   b. happy   c. elderly

3. Infection and disease spread quickly throughout field surgeries and hospitals, as few surgeons **sterilized** their equipment, rooms were not kept clean, and the same bandages were used repeatedly.
   a. bought　　**b.** disinfected　　**c.** used

4. She gained permission to pass through battle lines **tending** the wounded.
   a. caring for　　**b.** collecting　　**c.** counting

5. As a military nurse, Barton came to realize the importance of providing **aid** to the wounded.
   a. guns　　**b.** education　　**c.** help

6. It was she who founded the American Red Cross and who convinced more than a **dozen** countries to recognize the neutrality of the Red Cross flag.
   a. ten　　**b.** twelve　　**c.** fifteen

7. Barton quickly organized a network of contributors to **purchase** food and supplies.
   a. buy　　**b.** cook　　**c.** send

 LINKING PAST TO PRESENT　The American Red Cross is part of an international humanitarian agency called the International Federation of the Red Cross and Red Crescent Societies. This society is dedicated to helping wounded soldiers, civilians, and prisoners during times of war. In peacetime, it gives medical aid to people affected by natural disasters such as floods, earthquakes, epidemics, and famines. Today, the American Red Cross has more than 1.5 million volunteers.

REACT AND RESPOND　Have you or anyone you know ever been helped by the International Federation of the Red Cross and Red Crescent Societies? Why do you think volunteer organizations such as the Red Cross are important?

HISTORY MAKER: Abraham Lincoln

Carefully read the list of facts about Abraham Lincoln, the sixteenth president of the United States. Then choose the information you want from the list to write a paragraph about him on a separate piece of paper. Be sure to begin your paragraph with a topic sentence that states the main idea. Include transition words to guide the reader from one point to the next.

- considered one of the greatest leaders in history
- born in 1809 in a log cabin in Kentucky
- known as "Honest Abe" because he was so honest

- educated himself at home using library books
- trained himself to be a lawyer
- loved to read and write
- opposed slavery
- elected sixteenth president of the United States in 1860; re-elected in 1864
- led United States during the Civil War
- believed the most important goal of the Civil War was maintaining the Union
- said "A house divided against itself cannot stand. I believe this government cannot endure permanently half slave and half free."
- issued Emancipation Proclamation in 1863, freeing many slaves
- assassinated by John Wilkes Booth while attending a theater performance in 1865

Abraham Lincoln, the sixteenth president of the United States

Exchange your paragraph with a partner. Read your partner's paragraph and check it for correct grammar, punctuation, and capitalization.

LINKING PAST TO PRESENT Today the memories of Abraham Lincoln and George Washington are honored every February on a national holiday called Presidents' Day.

REACT AND RESPOND Are there any national holidays in your country that honor important political leaders? If so, how do you celebrate those days?

SKILL REVIEW: Sequencing

Read the short biography of Frederick Douglass and complete the exercise that follows.

Frederick Douglass

Frederick Douglass, runaway slave

1   Frederick Douglass was born a slave on February 7, 1817. His mother was also a slave. He never knew his white father. After being separated from his mother as an infant, Frederick lived with his grandmother on a Maryland plantation. When he was eight, his owner sent him to Baltimore to work as a servant in the household of Hugh Auld.

2   When Auld died in 1833, sixteen-year-old Frederick returned to the plantation to work as a field hand. After one failed attempt, he escaped to the North in 1838, finding work in New Bedford, Massachusetts. To fool slave hunters who might be following him, Frederick changed his last name from Bailey to Douglass.

3   Frederick Douglass soon became deeply involved in the abolitionist movement. After revealing in his 1845 autobiography that he was a runaway slave, he left the country. Otherwise he might have been recaptured.

4   During the next two years, Douglass earned enough money on an international speaking tour to buy his freedom. During the Civil War, Douglass served as an adviser to President Abraham Lincoln. He counseled Lincoln to arm former slaves so they could fight against the South. He personally recruited black soldiers for the Union army and made sure they were given equal pay. After the war, he held a number of important government positions, including U.S. minister to Haiti.

Put the list of events in the correct time order by numbering them from 1 to 9.

_____ **a.** During the Civil War, Douglass served as an adviser to President Abraham Lincoln.

_____ **b.** He became deeply involved in the abolitionist movement.

_____ **c.** Frederick was born a slave on February 7, 1817, and was separated from his mother.

_____ **d.** Frederick changed his last name from Bailey to Douglass and successfully escaped in 1838 to Massachusetts.

_____ **e.** He held a number of important government positions.

_____ **f.** Frederick bought his freedom.

_____ **g.** He went to Baltimore to work as a servant for Hugh Auld.

_____ **h.** He wrote his autobiography and left the country, fearing recapture.

_____ **i.** He tried to escape to the North but failed.

PUT IT TOGETHER

Discuss the questions.

1. In the 1850s, many people moved to California hoping to find gold. The population of California increased rapidly during that time. What are some reasons that population increases or decreases in a specific geographic area at a certain time? Give examples from your country.

2. Many Americans believe that Abraham Lincoln was the best president the United States has ever had. Who do you think is the best leader your country has ever had? Why?

3. In the United States, community service is an important concept. Many people volunteer in organizations such as the Red Cross. Are organizations that help people in need important in your country? Have you ever participated in one?

4. Has your country ever experienced a civil war? If so, what were the causes?

CHAPTER 4

INDUSTRIALIZATION AND THE FINAL FRONTIER

The Late 1800s

*I*n this chapter, you will read about the experiences of the pioneers, the Native Americans, and the immigrants in the late 1800s.

MAKE A CONNECTION

What was happening in your country in the late 1800s?

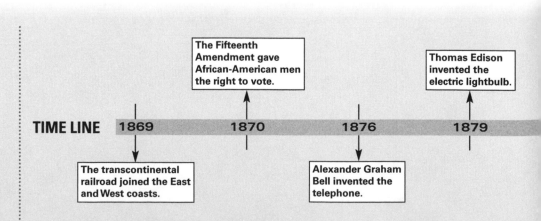

TIME LINE   1869   1870   1876   1879

The Fifteenth Amendment gave African-American men the right to vote.

Thomas Edison invented the electric lightbulb.

The transcontinental railroad joined the East and West coasts.

Alexander Graham Bell invented the telephone.

The United States in the Late 1800s

The late 1800s were a time of enormous growth for the United States.

Industrialization across the Country

Industrialization resulted in the development of large cities in the East and the final settlement of the West. After the Civil War, industry spread all across the nation and manufacturing dominated the economy. It was a golden age for American inventions. Between 1860 and 1890, the lightbulb, telephone, camera, typewriter, and phonograph were all invented. During this time, the railroad became the most important type of transportation, making it possible for people to travel and do business all over the country.

Final Westward Expansion

The final phase of westward expansion occurred during the late nineteenth century. At first, people had settled only those parts of the country that had trees and water. By 1865, several hundred thousand people had settled along the Pacific Coast, but very few people lived in the deserts, mountains, and plains of the West because of the harsh weather and lack of trees. This area was called the frontier.

In 1869, the nation's first cross-country railroad was completed, making the settlement of the frontier possible. In addition, the government gave free land to any citizen who agreed to live and work on it for five years. The men

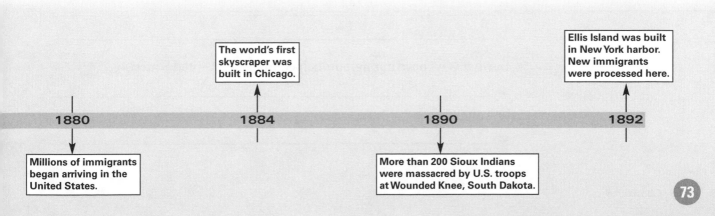

| | The world's first skyscraper was built in Chicago. | | Ellis Island was built in New York harbor. New immigrants were processed here. |

| **1880** | **1884** | **1890** | **1892** |

| Millions of immigrants began arriving in the United States. | | More than 200 Sioux Indians were massacred by U.S. troops at Wounded Knee, South Dakota. | |

and women who moved to the frontier were called pioneers. They were strong and brave people who were looking for a better life. The pioneers worked hard to settle the frontier, just as the colonists had done years before in the East.

As the white settlers moved west, the Native Americans who lived there were put on reservations. White settlers killed off many of the buffalo that the Native Americans had depended on for food and clothing. The way of life of the Native Americans was dying out.

Immigration

Immigrants from all over the world contributed to the growth of the United States during this time and helped shape the country economically, intellectually, and culturally. The largest wave of immigrants, almost 23 million, came to the United States between 1880 and 1924. Many worked in factories in the Northeast and Midwest. Others helped settle the West. Many aspects of American life, including religion, language, food, and music are products of the diverse nationalities that make up the United States.

CULTURE KERNEL

The Statue of Liberty was a gift from the people of France in 1886 to honor America's 100th birthday.

Answer the questions.

1. What were two important results of industrialization?

   a. _____

   b. _____

2. What dominated the economy at this time?

   _____

   _____

3. What were the two most important factors that encouraged the final settlement of the West?

   a. _____

   b. _____

4. As the white settlers moved west, what happened to the Native Americans who lived there?

   _____

   _____

5. In what ways have immigrants helped shape the United States?

   a. _____

   b. _____

   c. _____

The Transcontinental Railroad: Linking East to West

The construction of the first railroad that crossed the United States made settlement of the West much easier. However, the building of this railroad was expensive and dangerous. In this article, you will read about the difficult process of building the nation's first transcontinental railroad and how the railroad became an important means of transportation to the West.

BEFORE YOU READ

1. Look at the picture on page 76 and discuss why you think the construction of the transcontinental railroad helped destroy the huge herds of buffalo that roamed the Great Plains.

2. Look at the map and find the location where the Union Pacific and the Central Pacific railroads met.

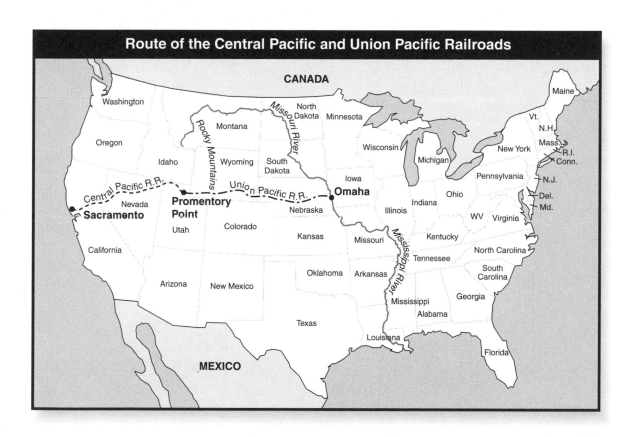

Route of the Central Pacific and Union Pacific Railroads

The Transcontinental Railroad: Linking East to West

1   The completion of the first transcontinental railroad in 1869 opened the West to settlers. For years Americans had talked about building a railroad that would connect the East and the West. In 1862, the government authorized two railroad companies, the Union Pacific and the Central Pacific, to construct a railroad line that would span the continent. The Union Pacific was to build westward from Omaha, Nebraska, and the Central Pacific was to build eastward from Sacramento, California.

2   Thousands of workers, including men who had fought in the Civil War, newly freed slaves, and immigrants, were hired to do the hard work of laying track across the deserts and through the mountains. The Central Pacific hired about 10,000 workers from China. They were paid $1 a day and worked twelve-hour shifts. Nine of every ten men who built the Central Pacific Railroad were Chinese. The Union Pacific also had a variety of workers including 8,000 to 10,000 Irish, German, and Italian immigrants. They worked twelve-hour shifts, just like the Central Pacific workers. Hundreds of workers died under the difficult conditions.

3   Seven years after construction began, the two lines met at Promontory Point, Utah. Crowds gathered to watch the May 10 joining of the Union Pacific and Central Pacific railroads. This first transcontinental railroad opened the West to supplies and resources from the East. It became the chief means of transportation for pioneers traveling west.

A group of men killing buffalo from the top of a railroad train

BUILD YOUR TEST-TAKING SKILLS

Circle the letter of the choice that best completes each sentence.

1. The passage mainly discusses _____.
   a. the advantages and disadvantages of transcontinental railroads
   b. methods of transportation in the West
   c. why Civil War veterans wanted to work on the railroad
   d. the building of the first transcontinental railroad

2. The author mentions all of the following groups as working on the building of the transcontinental railroad except _____.
   a. immigrants
   b. Native Americans
   c. Civil War veterans
   d. newly freed slaves

3. The transcontinental railroad was important because _____.
   a. it opened the West to settlers
   b. it took seven years to build
   c. it ended the Civil War
   d. workers were paid $1 per day

4. The word *connect* in the second sentence of the first paragraph is closest in meaning to _____.
   a. pay
   b. build
   c. join
   d. hire

CHECK YOUR COMPREHENSION

Mark each item true (T) or false (F).

_____ 1. The Union Pacific railroad company refused to hire immigrants.

_____ 2. The first transcontinental railroad in the United States was completed in 1869.

_____ 3. The workers laid the railroad tracks only on flat land.

_____ 4. Workers for both the Union Pacific and the Central Pacific worked twelve-hour shifts.

_____ 5. The conditions for railroad workers was so dangerous that many died.

BUILD YOUR DICTIONARY SKILLS

Use a dictionary to identify the correct definition and part of speech for each of these words from Reading 1. Be sure to look for the definition that fits the context of the word.

1. line (_____) _____

2. span (_____) _____

3. track (_____) _____

4. shift (_____) _____

5. supplies (_____) _____

6. chief (_____) _____

Fireworks over the Brooklyn Bridge

LINKING PAST TO PRESENT

For centuries, Native Americans had depended on buffalo for food, clothing, tools, and fuel. In the early 1800s, there were about 60 million buffalo, but in the 1830s, white settlers killed many of the buffalo, eventually reducing their number to less than 1,000. The construction of the transcontinental railroad also contributed to the massacre of the buffalo as railroad workers killed buffalo for food. In May 1894, Congress passed a law that made the hunting of buffalo illegal. This was the first step by the U.S. government to protect an animal that earlier American settlers had tried to eliminate. Today, about 30,000 buffalo live in protected areas and on private ranches.

REACT AND RESPOND What role do you think government should play in protecting animals? Are any animals facing extinction in your country? What is being done to try to save them?

READING 2 **Women on the Lone Prairie**

During the late nineteenth century, many people believed it was America's duty to settle the West. As you will see in this reading, life for the pioneers on the Great Plains was difficult, and they suffered many dangers and hardships. The harsh climate and the lack of water and trees were constant problems. The pioneers also had to deal with isolation and loneliness. Most pioneer women were courageous and determined, which helped them survive the difficult years of settling the prairie.

BEFORE YOU READ

One of the best things you can do to improve your reading skills is to *preview* an article before you read it. When you preview an article, you examine certain parts of the article before you read it carefully. This usually involves looking at the article's title, subtitle, pictures, charts, and headings for information about the article. Previewing will give you a general idea of what the article is about. Knowing the general idea of the article will help you understand it. Previewing will also give you clues about the organization of the information in the article and the main ideas. Finally, previewing will help you determine the level of difficulty of the writing.

Here are some steps to follow when you preview an article. Use these steps to preview Reading 2, which begins on page 81.

1. Look at the title of the article and write it on the line below. The title usually tells you what an article is about. What do you think this article will be about?

   _____

   _____

2. Read the subtitle and write it on the line below. The subtitle usually summarizes the main idea of an article. What do you think the main idea of this article might be?

   _____

   _____

3. The headings that appear throughout the article give you more clues about the content of each section. Write the headings on the lines below and predict what each section will be about.

   a. _____

   _____

   b. _____

   _____

4. Read the first and last paragraphs of the article. The first paragraph is usually an introduction to an article and will tell you the purpose of the article. The last paragraph usually gives the conclusion or summarizes the article. These two paragraphs are usually important because they provide you with a general overview of the whole article.

5. Examine the picture and map in the article and read the captions that go with them. These visual aids often highlight important concepts. Reading 2 contains one map and one picture. Guess why the author included them.

6. Read the first sentence of each paragraph. This is often the topic sentence and will give you the main idea of the paragraph.

7. Now read the article one time all the way through. Do not stop reading to look up words in the dictionary and do not worry about parts that you do not understand. The purpose of the first reading is simply to give you a general sense of the article and to prepare you for a more careful reading.

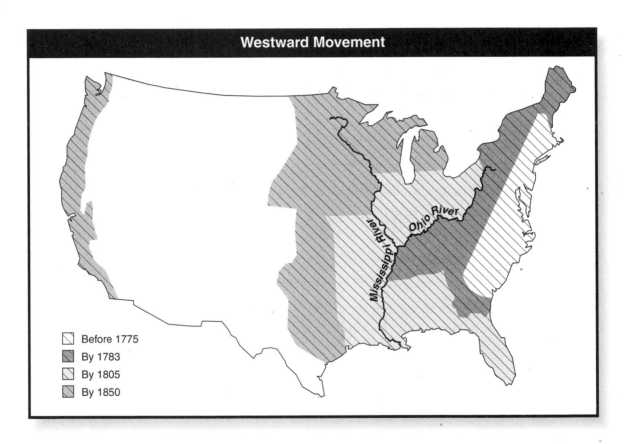

This map shows the settling of territories between 1775 and 1850.

Women on the Lone Prairie

by Sean McCollum

Women Settlers Tell What It Took to Conquer the American Frontier

*A **pioneer woman collects buffalo chips to use for fuel.***

1   Much of the popular history of the Wild West focuses on gunfighters and gunfights, cowboys and Indians. But the experiences of women and families paint a more accurate picture of America's westward expansion. It was ordinary settlers who helped settle a desolate land.

2   The Great Plains extend from the Missouri River in the east to the Rocky Mountains in the west, and from Canada in the north to the Texas Panhandle in the south. The Great Plains were one of the toughest, most inhospitable regions of America yet to be settled. It had only two natural resources: grass and soil. But after better lands were gone, settlers from the East and immigrants from overseas saw the prairie as a place where they could escape poverty and own a piece of land.

3   The settling of the prairie began in the 1850s. Then, following the Civil War (1861–1865), it accelerated. In 1860, for example, 28,000 white settlers lived in the Nebraska Territory. Seven years later, when Nebraska became the thirty-seventh state, the population was 100,000. To encourage settlement of the West, the U.S. government passed the Homestead Act in 1862. This act offered up to 160 acres of free land to any settlers—or homesteaders, as they were called—who agreed to develop the land and live on it for five years.

4   Pioneer families worked together to settle the harsh land, with women doing the same work as men. Their stories, taken from diaries and letters, give us an idea about the social history of this time.

PEOPLE IN GRASS HOUSES

5   Finding housing was the greatest challenge to the prairie pioneers because there were so few trees for lumber. So what to build with?

6   Grass and soil—called sod—were the only materials available. Families dug homes, called dugouts, into the sides of hills. Others built "soddies"—houses made of sod. "The typical sod cabin was constructed by stacking the sod bricks, one layer after another," describes one historian. "Laid with grass side down, the blocks were placed side by side to form walls two feet thick. . . . In all, it took nearly one full acre of prairie turf to provide enough bricks for a one-room soddy."

7   Homesteaders found value in the unlikeliest things. "[My husband] set the cook stove on the ground near the creek," Emma Smith from Kansas recalled. "But

(continues on next page)

what could we burn for fuel? There was not a tree or bush in sight. . . . But I soon learned . . . how and what to gather to make a fire. 'Chips' (dried manure) were plentiful, as the plains had for years been an open range, first for buffalo, then for cattle. . . . The sod house and cow chips were two great factors in making possible the settlement of this country."

8   The homesteaders' first winter was often their most difficult. Rachel and Abraham Calof's in-laws had to move into their soddie for the winter because they didn't have any fuel.

9   "At this time, my in-laws had twelve chickens, and Abe and I also had twelve. If there had been [an outdoor chicken coop], we would have lost the flock because the temperature outside was forty degrees below zero. . . . Each family was to keep its chickens under its bed. Also, there was a calf to be accommodated inside. This is how five human beings and twenty-five animals faced the beginning of the fierce winter of the plains in a twelve-by-fourteen-foot shack."

TRIALS, TRIBULATIONS, AND THE PIONEER SPIRIT

10   The fierce weather of the Great Plains could break the will and hopes of a homesteader in an afternoon.

11   "The wheat grew well [in 1900]," remembered Rachel Calof, "and, at last, was ready for cutting. On a fine clear morning [my husband] . . . made . . . preparations . . . to reap the golden harvest. But, shortly before noon, a dark cloud suddenly boiled up in the sky. Then suddenly the hailstorm, the scourge of the prairie farmer, was upon us. It was so strong that in a few minutes practically all for which we had suffered and labored was destroyed."

12   During dry summers there were more problems, such as prairie fires, tornadoes, and plagues of locusts that ate everything in their path, even the clothing off people's backs.

13   A homesteader's isolated life presented dangers of its own. The nearest neighbor, doctor, or town was often miles away. Sometimes, loneliness drove settlers crazy. And isolation could turn common events into big problems, as homesteader Annette Lecleve Botkin recalled.

14   "My parents settled in Kansas, in 1873. Their house was three miles from the nearest neighbor.

15   "It was the last of July, and my father was thinking of the long winter ahead. . . . The little house had to be kept warm, for there were a couple of little children already in the home, and another on the way. So my father rose early and started on his all-day trip . . . to get a load of wood. . . .

16   "He had no sooner gotten out of sight, than my mother knew . . . that it was time [to give birth]. Now that was a terrifying situation. Alone with two babies, not a neighbor nor doctor to be gotten.

17   "So my mother got the baby clothes together on a chair by the bed, water, and scissors and what else was needed to take care of the baby; drew a bucket of fresh water from a sixty-foot well; made some bread-and-butter sandwiches; set out some milk for the babies. At about noon she had a fine baby boy. My father arrived home about dusk with a big load of wood and . . . he found a very uncomfortable but brave and thankful mother."

18   By the 1890s, the Great Plains were tamed. After two decades of war, Indian tribes had been forced onto reservations. "Soddies" were replaced with wooden frame houses. Towns and farms dotted

what had so recently been an unbroken sea of grass.

19 "It might seem a cheerless life," said one woman, reflecting on the challenges of her pioneer days, "but there were compensations: the thrill of conquering a new country; the wonderful atmosphere; the attraction of the prairie, which simply gets into your blood and makes you dissatisfied away from it; the low-lying hills and the unobstructed view of the horizon; and the fleecy clouds driven by the never-failing winds. The pioneer spirit was continuous in our family."

BUILD YOUR READING SKILLS: Recognizing Main Ideas

Check (✓) the topics that are discussed in Reading 2.

_____ 1. the Homestead Act

_____ 2. the location of the Great Plains

_____ 3. problems faced during the summers

_____ 4. how pioneers solved housing problems

_____ 5. treatment of Native Americans on the Great Plains

_____ 6. the problem of isolation on the prairie

_____ 7. the history of the settling of the prairie

_____ 8. natural resources of the Great Plains

_____ 9. education for children of pioneers

CHECK YOUR COMPREHENSION

Circle the letter of the choice that best completes each sentence.

1. The Great Plains are bordered by _____ in the north.
   a. the Missouri River
   b. the Rocky Mountains
   c. Canada
   d. the Texas Panhandle

2. Nebraska became a state in _____.
   a. 1850
   b. 1861
   c. 1865
   d. 1867

3. The Homestead Act _____.
   a. encouraged settlement of the West
   b. offered free land to Native Americans
   c. made Nebraska a state
   d. ended the Civil War

4. Dugouts and soddies are _____.
   a. farming techniques
   b. types of housing
   c. chicken coops
   d. methods of transportation

5. Pioneers used _____ to make fires.
   a. branches from trees
   b. bushes
   c. buffalo chips
   d. sod

6. _____ threatened the crops of pioneers.
   a. Fires
   b. Locusts
   c. Hailstorms
   d. All of the above

7. The greatest challenge prairie pioneers faced was _____.
   a. farming
   b. housing
   c. schooling
   d. cooking

CULTURE KERNEL

The invention of barbed wire changed life in the western United States almost as much as the railroad did. Barbed wire fencing ended the open range. It gave small farmers greater protection.

EXPAND YOUR VOCABULARY

*Decide whether the pairs of words are synonyms or antonyms. If they are synonyms, circle **S**. If they are antonyms, circle **A**.*

1. accurate	correct	S	A
2. desolate	barren	S	A
3. inhospitable	hospitable	S	A
4. isolated	secluded	S	A
5. terrifying	frightening	S	A
6. plentiful	scarce	S	A
7. thrill	excitement	S	A
8. prairie	plains	S	A

BUILD YOUR READING SKILLS: Understanding Transitions

Read the sentences and underline the transitions. Write the transition word(s) on the line and identify the type of relationship it signifies. Refer to the chart on page 36.

1. The settling of the prairie began in the 1850s. Then, following the Civil War (1861–1865), it accelerated.

   Transition: _____ Type of relationship: _____

2. In 1860, for example, 28,000 white settlers lived in the Nebraska Territory.

   Transition: _____ Type of relationship: _____

3. If there had been [an outdoor chicken coop], we would have lost the flock because the temperature outside was forty degrees below zero.

   Transition: _____ Type of relationship: _____

   Transition: _____ Type of relationship: _____

4. But, shortly before noon, a dark cloud suddenly boiled up in the sky. Then suddenly the hailstorm, the scourge of the prairie farmer, was upon us.

   Transition: _____ Type of relationship: _____

   Transition: _____ Type of relationship: _____

5. The little house had to be kept warm, for there were a couple of little children already in the home, and another on the way.

   Transition: _____ Type of relationship: _____

6. "It might seem a cheerless life," said one woman, "but there were compensations: the thrill of conquering a new country; the wonderful atmosphere . . ."

   Transition: _____ Type of relationship: _____

TALK ABOUT IT

What do you think were the most difficult aspects of living on the prairie?

WRITE ABOUT IT

Do you think you would have made a good pioneer? Why or why not? What aspects of pioneer life would you like? What aspects would you dislike? Answer these questions in paragraph form on a separate piece of paper.

A pioneer is a person who paves the way for others to follow. Pioneers often suffer great hardships to achieve their goals. The adventurous pioneer spirit of the American West has not died out. In the late 1800s, the new frontier was the territory west of the Mississippi River. Today, pioneers are exploring the depths of the ocean and the expanse of outer space.

REACT AND RESPOND In what other areas are pioneers exploring? What people do you consider to be modern-day pioneers?

READING 3   **Walking the White Road**

In this passage, you will read about the problems the Native Americans faced after the white settlers arrived in the New World. The article begins with an introduction and contains a series of excerpts written by Native Americans. Each excerpt is followed by an exercise.

Walking the White Road
by David Oliver Relin

1   For 400 years after Columbus arrived in the New World, much of American history involved warfare between white settlers and American Indians [Native Americans]. By the end of the nineteenth century, nearly every American Indian had either been killed in battle, died from disease, or been moved onto reservations.

2   By 1890, many settlers had moved west to cultivate the land of the open prairie. They hunted and killed off most of the great buffalo herds and built railroads and wire fences throughout the West.

3   With the Indian wars over, the U.S. government tried to assimilate, or fit, the surviving tribes into white society. Through laws, persuasion, education—and force—the government began the business of reinventing the Indian. American

Indians called this painful process "learning to walk the white road." In the following excerpts, Indians tell in their own words the story of the dramatic transformation of Indian life.

The three teepees

Reservation Life

By 1880, about 300,000 Native Americans had been forced to live on reservations. It was difficult for Native Americans to adjust to their new life. In this excerpt from his autobiography, one Native American describes adjusting to reservation life as a teenager.

> We had everything to learn about the white man's way of life. We had come to an area that was new to us, where wind and rain and rivers and heat and cold and even some of the plants and animals were different from what we had always known. We had to learn to live by farming instead of by hunting and trading; we had to learn from people who did not speak our language or try to learn it . . . though they expected us to learn theirs. We had to learn to cut our hair short, and to wear close-fitting clothes made of dull-colored cloth, and to live in houses, though we knew that our long braids of hair and embroidered robes and moccasins and tall, round lodges were more beautiful.
>
> —Carl Sweezy, Arapaho

CHECK YOUR COMPREHENSION

Complete the chart with items from the list.

live in tall, round lodges   hunting and trading

dress in close-fitting clothes   dress in embroidered robes

live in houses   wear long braids

farming   wear hair short

DIFFERENCES IN ARAPAHO LIFESTYLE		
	Old Way of Life	**New Way of Life**
Food		
Hair		
Clothing		
Housing		

Becoming White

In 1879, a school opened in Carlisle, Pennsylvania. Its purpose was to expose Indian students to white culture. Similar schools opened throughout the country. In 1882, a student wrote about life at Carlisle.

> They told us that Indian ways were bad. They said we must get civilized. I remember that word. It means "be like the white man." I am willing to be like the white man, but I did not believe Indian ways were wrong. Their books told how bad the Indians had been to the white men—burning towns and killing women and children. But I had seen white men do that to Indians. We all wore white man's clothes and ate white man's food and went to white man's churches and spoke white man's talk. And so after a while we began to say Indians were bad. We laughed at our own people and their [customs]. I tried to learn the lessons.
>
> —Sun Elk, Hopi

WRITE ABOUT IT

Pretend you are a Hopi student attending school in Carlisle. On a separate piece of paper, write a letter to your parents about what you are learning and how you feel about it.

A Way of Life Passes

By 1900, traditional Indian life was near extinction. Indians rarely lived as hunters or practiced their traditional beliefs. In 1926, an elderly woman looked back at the passing of a way of life.

> I am an old woman now. The buffaloes and black-tail deer are gone, and our ways are almost gone. Sometimes I find it hard to believe that I ever lived them. My little son grew up in the white man's school. He can read books, and he owns cattle and has a farm. We no longer live in an earth lodge, but in a house with chimneys; and my son's wife cooks by a stove. I cannot forget our old ways. Sometimes in the evening, in the shadows, I see again our village, with smoke curling upward from the earth lodges; and in the river's roar I hear the yells of the warriors. . . . It is but an old woman's dream . . . tears come into my eyes. Our Indian life, I know, is gone forever.
>
> —Buffalo Bird Woman, Hidatsa

TALK ABOUT IT

Do you think it is sad when a way of life passes? What are the advantages and disadvantages of giving up an old way of life and adopting a new one? In small groups, make a list of the advantages and disadvantages.

EXPAND YOUR VOCABULARY

Match each word from the reading with its meaning.

_____ 1. assimilate   **a.** land for American Indians to live on

_____ 2. cultivate   **b.** adapting

_____ 3. extinction   **c.** fit in

_____ 4. reservation   **d.** dying out

_____ 5. transformation   **e.** prepare land for growing crops

_____ 6. adjusting   **f.** change

TALK ABOUT IT

In small groups, discuss an event in the history of your country that makes you feel proud or embarrassed.

WRITE ABOUT IT

On a separate piece of paper, write a letter to a friend from a different culture describing an event that is important in the history of your country. Explain how you feel about this event.

 LINKING PAST TO PRESENT English borrowed many words from the Native American languages, such as *moccasins*, *pecans*, *moose*, and *raccoon*. Common place names such as *Chicago*, *Omaha*, *Tampa*, *Utah*, *Texas*, and *Kentucky* are also from Native American languages.

REACT AND RESPOND What words has English borrowed from your language? What words has your language borrowed from English?

READING 4 **Identity Crisis**

Native Americans were not the only people who had to adapt to a new way of life. The millions of immigrants who moved to the United States from different countries also needed to adapt to a new culture. Coming to find better jobs or better land to farm or to escape religious or political persecution, starvation, or war, these people have made significant economic, intellectual, and cultural contributions to the growth of the United States. In this article, you will read about what it was like to be an immigrant in the late 1800s.

BEFORE YOU READ

Study the graph of European immigration between 1870 and 1920. Then answer the questions.

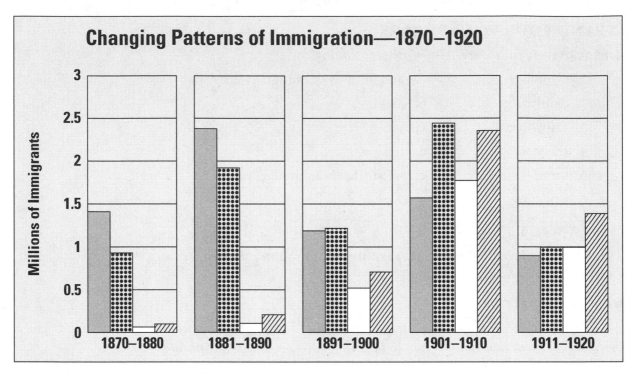

Changing Patterns of Immigration—1870–1920

Millions of Immigrants

Northwestern Europe: Great Britain, Ireland, Scandinavia, The Netherlands, Belgium, Luxembourg, Switzerland, France

Central Europe: Germany, Poland, Austria-Hungary

Eastern Europe: Russia, Romania, Bulgaria, Turkey

Southern Europe: Italy, Spain, Portugal, Greece

1. How many eastern Europeans entered the United States between 1901 and 1910? _____

2. In what years did almost the same number of northwestern Europeans and central Europeans arrive in the United States? _____

3. What years saw the largest increase in the number of immigrants from southern Europe? _____

4. What was the immigration trend between 1911 and 1920? _____

Identity Crisis
by Tod Olson

1   Since the first settlers arrived in America in the seventeenth century, more than 60 million immigrants have had to decide what it means to be an American. The greatest number of immigrants—some 23 million of them—arrived on these shores between 1880 and 1920. They came from all over the world, but the majority were from small villages in Poland, Russia, Italy, and elsewhere in Europe. In trying to assimilate, or fit in, the children of immigrants were caught between two worlds.

2   These children worked hard to adapt. They learned English and explored American attractions such as baseball and the movies. But often, their efforts to assimilate left the older generation troubled. Parents did not want their children to lose touch with the Old World and tried to steer them toward European games, European friends, European languages. These efforts usually failed. To most immigrant teenagers, the old family traditions were just that—old.

3   The following excerpts are from memoirs and letters written by teenagers in immigrant families at the turn of the century. They describe how these young people solved the problem of becoming American.

Immigrants arrive in New York.

(continues on next page)

SPEAK ENGLISH

A Jewish newspaper in New York called The Daily Forward *published an advice column, in which immigrants asked for help with problems they had in adjusting to American life. These immigrants were from Europe and spoke a language called Yiddish.*

Worthy Editor:

I am sure that the problem I'm writing about affects many Jewish homes. My parents, who have been readers of your paper for years, came from Europe. They have five sons.

We, the five brothers, always speak English to each other. Our parents know English too, but they speak only Yiddish, not just among themselves, but to us, too, and even to our American friends who come to visit us. We beg them not to speak Yiddish in the presence of our friends, but they always do.

Imagine, even when we go with our father to buy something in a store on Fifth Avenue, New York, he insists on speaking Yiddish. We are not ashamed of our parents, God forbid, but they ought to know where it's proper and where it's not. They want to keep only to their old ways and don't want to take up our new ways.

We beg you to express your opinion, and if possible, send us your answer in English because we can't read Yiddish.

The five brothers

Dear Brothers:

We see no crime in the parents speaking Yiddish to their sons. The Yiddish language is dear to them. It may also be that they are ashamed to speak their imperfect English among strangers so they prefer to use their mother tongue.

The Editors

A NAME IS NOT A SHIRT

Immigrants sometimes changed their names to make them sound more American. As Italian-American Leonard Covello says in his memoir, this could be an emotional issue.

One day I came home from school with a report card for my father to sign. My father glanced over the marks on the report card and was about to sign it. However, he paused with the pen in his hand.

"What is this? Leonard Covello! What happened to the 'i' in Coviello?"

"Mrs. Cutter took it out," I explained. "Every time she pronounced Coviello, it came out Covello. So she took out the 'i.' What difference does it make?" I said. "It's more American." At that age, I felt that anything that made a name less foreign was an improvement.

For a moment my father sat there. Then with a shrug of resignation, he signed the report card. My mother now entered the argument. "How is it possible to do this to a name? You will have to tell your teacher that a name cannot be changed just like that."

"Mamma, you don't understand."

"What is there to understand? A person's honor is in his name. He never changes it. A name is not a shirt or a piece of underwear."

"You just don't understand!"

"Will you stop saying that!" my mother insisted. "Now that you have become Americanized you understand everything and I understand nothing."

I beckoned to [my friend] Vito and we walked downstairs into the street.

Somehow the joy of childhood had seeped out of our lives.

CHECK YOUR COMPREHENSION

Answer the questions.

1. In "Speak English!" why are the five brothers upset with their parents?
2. How do the children feel when their parents speak Yiddish in front of their friends?
3. Why do you think the sons want to speak English? Why do the parents want to speak Yiddish?
4. What do you think the title "A Name Is Not a Shirt" means?
5. How did Leonard's father react when he saw Leonard's report card?
6. What was Leonard's mother's reaction?
7. Why did Leonard want to change his last name?

EXPAND YOUR VOCABULARY

Complete each sentence with a word from the list. Change the form if necessary.

adapt   tradition   advice   pause

insist   proper   recall

1. My parents gave me good _____ about which university to attend.

2. Sometimes it is not _____ to call an adult by his or her first name.

3. The student _____ when he came to a word he did not understand in the reading.

4. It is a _____ in this country for women to get married in white dresses.

5. Sometimes it is difficult for immigrants to _____ to the culture of their new country.

6. The teacher _____ that we do our homework in ink.

7. I'm sorry but I can't _____ the name of the restaurant.

BUILD YOUR READING SKILLS: Using Context to Understand Vocabulary

When you read, it is not always necessary to know the exact meaning of an unfamiliar word or phrase. Sometimes figuring out the general idea is enough to allow you to understand the meaning of a sentence. Part of becoming a good reader is being able to determine when you need to know the exact definition or when a general idea is enough.

Using clues such as punctuation, grammar, and the general meaning of the sentence, try to figure out the meaning of the words in bold type. Write an approximate definition or synonym of that word. Do not use your dictionary.

1. In trying to **assimilate,** or fit in, the children of immigrants were caught between two worlds.

   _____

2. Parents did not want their children to lose touch with the Old World and tried to **steer** them toward European games, European friends, and European languages.

   _____

3. The following **excerpts** are from memoirs and letters written by teenagers in immigrant families at the turn of the century.

   _____

4. It may also be that they are **ashamed** to speak their imperfect English among strangers so they prefer to use their mother **tongue.**

   _____

   _____

5. My father **glanced** over the marks on the report card and was about to sign it.

   _____

6. I **beckoned** to [my friend] Vito and we walked downstairs into the street.

   _____

TALK ABOUT IT

1. Should people give up their language when they move to a new country? Why or why not?

2. Why do you think children are more willing than their parents to adopt the language of a new country?

3. What else besides language is difficult for immigrants to give up?

4. How important are family names in your culture? Would your parents or grandparents be upset if you changed your family name?

WRITE ABOUT IT

Choose one of the discussion questions from the exercise Talk About It. *On a separate piece of paper, write a one-paragraph answer to the question.*

LINKING PAST TO PRESENT While the people of most countries share a cultural history, the people of the United States do not. In fact, almost everyone living in the United States or their ancestors came from another country. The United States is truly a country of immigrants.

REACT AND RESPOND How do you think the multicultural population of the United States has affected the country's growth? What are the advantages and disadvantages of such a heterogeneous population? Does your country have people from many different cultural backgrounds? If so, what are they? How have they affected the growth of the country?

HISTORY MAKER: Thomas Edison

Carefully read the list of facts about the great inventor Thomas Edison. Then choose the information you want from the list to write a paragraph about him on a separate piece of paper. Be sure to begin your paragraph with a topic sentence that states the main idea. Include transition words to guide the reader from one point to the next.

Thomas Edison, the great inventor

- was the greatest inventor in history

- born in 1847 in Milan, Ohio

- went to school for only three months

- was a very curious child, always asking "why?"

- changed the lives of millions of people

- invented electric light, phonograph, and 1,093 other inventions

- helped develop motion pictures by combining phonograph and camera

- helped improve the telephone, typewriter, electric generator, electric trains

- registered more than 1,093 patents

- was independent and liked to work alone

- was a hard worker—worked long hours at a time with no break even for sleep

- married twice; both wives complained that he spent too much time in his laboratories

- enjoyed his work more than anything else

- died in 1931

Exchange your paragraph with a partner. Read your partner's paragraph and check it for correct grammar, punctuation, and capitalization.

CULTURE KERNEL

In 1899, Charles Duell, the head of the U.S. Patent Office stated, "Everything that can be invented has been invented!"

SKILL REVIEW: Using Context to Understand Vocabulary

Read the paragraph about the artist Mary Cassatt and complete the exercise that follows. Use clues such as punctuation and grammar to help you figure out the meaning of the words in bold type.

Mary Cassatt

1   Mary Cassatt was the first important female American artist. Although she was born in 1844 in Allegheny, Pennsylvania, Cassatt spent much of her career living in France. She **adopted** the Impressionist style of painting, and she was the only American artist invited to **exhibit** her work at Impressionist exhibitions in Paris. Cassatt was greatly influenced in her work by the French painter Edgar Degas, who became her close friend. As she grew older and her style **matured**, she became influenced by the woodcuts of Japanese artists. Many of her paintings explored the life of women doing **ordinary** things such as drinking tea and writing letters. She is perhaps best known today for her many paintings of mothers with their young children. Unfortunately, she lost her eyesight in her later years. During that time, however, she played a major role in encouraging American collectors to buy Impressionist art. Cassatt died in 1926.

"Tea" by Mary Cassatt

Write an approximate definition or synonym of the words in bold. Do not use your dictionary.

1. adopted _____

2. exhibit _____

3. matured _____

4. ordinary _____

PUT IT TOGETHER

Discuss the questions.

1. On average, an American moves six times in his or her adult life. People are constantly changing jobs, houses, and locations in the search for something better. Is this true in your country? Why or why not?

2. An English proverb says that "necessity is the mother of invention." Think about some of the inventions mentioned in this chapter and discuss the necessities that caused them to be invented.

3. The arts in America reflect the way that cultures have mixed during three centuries of immigration. Discuss any ways you know that American music, dance, movies, painting, photography, literature, theater, or fashion have been influenced by the mixture of cultures.

4. What are some typical problems that immigrants face besides language? What kinds of things do you think are hardest for them to adjust to? What advice would you give people coming to the United States to visit or live?

CHAPTER 5

A NEW CENTURY

*The
First
Two
Decades*

*I*n this chapter, you will read about the powerful effects of rapid growth on American society at the beginning of the twentieth century.

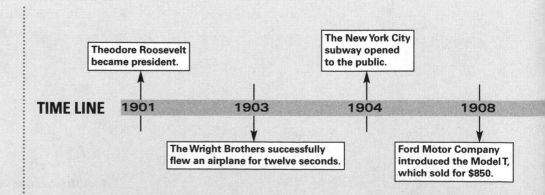

TIME LINE

Theodore Roosevelt became president.

The New York City subway opened to the public.

1901   1903   1904   1908

The Wright Brothers successfully flew an airplane for twelve seconds.

Ford Motor Company introduced the Model T, which sold for $850.

The United States in 1900–1920

By 1900, the United States had expanded from the Atlantic to the Pacific Ocean and had created one of the most powerful economies in the world. Several factors helped this rapid growth: (1) A rich supply of natural resources provided raw materials needed for industrialization; (2) an increase in birthrate and immigration provided a large pool of workers; and (3) strong communication and transportation systems helped business thrive.

Social Problems and Reform

Unfortunately, new growth also brought problems. Some people became extremely wealthy, but others remained terribly poor. Factory workers, even young children, worked twelve hours a day in dangerous conditions but were paid very little. Millions of immigrants crowded into cities filled with crime and poverty. Most blacks were prevented from voting, and women still could not vote. All over the country, people realized that it was time for a change. The result was that a new reform movement, called the Progressive movement, was born. The Progressives focused on the problems resulting from industrialization, immigration, political corruption, and big business.

War in Europe/Women at Home

While reform was going on in the United States, World War I broke out in Europe in 1914. In World War I, the airplane, invented just a decade earlier, was used as a weapon of war for the first time. At first, the United States tried

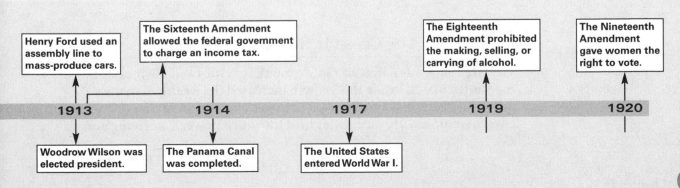

Henry Ford used an assembly line to mass-produce cars.

The Sixteenth Amendment allowed the federal government to charge an income tax.

The Eighteenth Amendment prohibited the making, selling, or carrying of alcohol.

The Nineteenth Amendment gave women the right to vote.

1913   1914   1917   1919   1920

Woodrow Wilson was elected president.

The Panama Canal was completed.

The United States entered World War I.

to stay out of the war, but as the war continued, it began to affect the American people. In 1917, Americans united in support of the government's decision to enter the war. Women filled many of the jobs left by men who went to fight. The contributions of women to the war effort resulted in public support for their right to vote, and in 1920, women finally won that right.

Growth of Popular Culture

The country's rapid growth also affected the arts, education, and leisure time. Music thrived, and a new type of music called jazz was developed by black Americans. Education was seen as a way to get ahead in life, and the number of high school and college students increased significantly. The idea of "going out and having fun" gained popularity, too. Amusement parks and movie theaters became popular, as did outdoor sports such as baseball and bicycling. More than ever before, a new and distinctly American culture was emerging. It was informal, optimistic, and socially mobile.

Answer the questions.

1. What factors helped the United States grow so quickly?

   a. _____

   b. _____

   c. _____

2. What areas of life did the Progressives try to reform?

   a. _____

   b. _____

   c. _____

   d. _____

3. What other areas of American life were affected by rapid growth?

   a. _____

   b. _____

   c. _____

READING 1 The Crusade for Social Reform

The late 1800s was a time of rapid growth for cities and businesses in the United States. While this growth increased the wealth of many people, it also caused problems. There was corruption in the government, and big businesses held too much power. The living and working conditions of city dwellers got worse. Many people began to worry about the serious problems in American society. As a result, a reform movement, called the Progressive movement, was born in the early 1900s. In this article you will read about the writers who exposed corruption in government, politics, and business and helped bring about social change.

The Crusade for Social Reform

1   The type of news that was reported changed during the early years of the twentieth century. The people who practiced this new kind of journalism were called *muckrakers* because they found news by raking through the "muck" or mud of dishonest business practices. Muckrakers were the first real investigative journalists. Their specialty was exposing the cheating and corruption of people in powerful places.

2   One of the first and most important muckrakers was Lincoln Steffens, who wrote a series of articles called "The Shame of the Cities" between 1901 and 1906. These articles uncovered corruption in city governments all over the country. One article revealed that the Minneapolis police department took bribes from criminals. Following Steffens's example, other writers began to investigate bribery in the nation's largest corporations and even the U.S. Senate.

3   Muckraker Upton Sinclair took on the U.S. food industry. In his 1906 novel, *The Jungle,* Sinclair described in realistic detail the revolting working conditions in Chicago meatpacking plants. He wrote about how garbage, including dead rats, was sometimes packed in cans along with the meat. The public outrage caused by Sinclair's book led directly to passage of the Pure Food and Drug and Meat Inspection acts, which established quality standards and a system of government inspection.

After President Theodore Roosevelt read about the terrible conditions of the meatpacking industry, he was so disgusted that he decided to become a vegetarian.

BUILD YOUR TEST-TAKING SKILLS

Circle the letter of the choice that best completes each sentence or answers the question.

1. The article mentions Lincoln Steffens and Upton Sinclair as examples of _____.

   a. businessmen
   b. politicians
   c. muckrakers
   d. policemen

2. You can conclude from the article that the Chicago meatpacking plants _____.

   a. didn't meet the standards that the Pure Food and Drug and Meat Inspection acts later set
   b. met the standards that the Pure Food and Drug and Meat Inspection acts later set
   c. wanted the public to know about the conditions of the meatpacking process
   d. were a shining example of sanitary meatpacking conditions

3. The main goal of the muckrakers was to _____.
   a. write exciting novels
   b. expose cheating and corruption in society
   c. bribe police officers
   d. none of the above

4. "The Shame of the Cities" was a series of articles dealing with _____.

   a. the conditions of meatpacking plants in cities all over the country
   b. the causes of the growth of U.S. cities
   c. the problems immigrants faced in large cities
   d. corruption in city governments across the United States

5. Which of the following can you conclude from the article?
   a. Before the twentieth century, there was little investigative journalism.
   b. Muckrakers were all honest, upright citizens.
   c. There were very few corrupt people in powerful positions.
   d. Many police departments across the country took bribes from criminals.

EXPAND YOUR VOCABULARY

Decide whether the pairs of words are synonyms or antonyms. If they are synonyms, circle S. If they are antonyms, circle A.

1.	revolting	appealing	S	A
2.	uncovered	revealed	S	A
3.	dishonest	corrupt	S	A
4.	outrage	approval	S	A
5.	investigate	research	S	A
6.	directly	indirectly	S	A
7.	realistic	unrealistic	S	A

LINKING PAST TO PRESENT Throughout their history, Americans have worked for social change and reform. Progressive ideas have been a key to American democracy. Today, many people are still concerned about corruption in the government, the power of big business, and the social conditions of the underprivileged.

REACT AND RESPOND What problems do you think people face when they work for social change and reform? Are people in your country concerned about political corruption? What about the power of big business? Social welfare? How successful have reform movements been in your country?

READING 2   The Wright Brothers: First Flight

For many years, inventors from all over the world tried to build flying machines, but none of them were successful. In 1903, Orville and Wilbur Wright, bicycle mechanics from Dayton, Ohio, succeeded where all others had failed. In this reading, you will learn about their historic flight.

The Wright Brothers: First Flight

1   On the morning of December 17, 1903, near the village of Kitty Hawk, North Carolina, brothers Orville and Wilbur Wright did something that humans had never done before: They flew in a heavier-than-air machine. On their first attempt, with Orville at the controls, the plane traveled 120 feet in the air, staying aloft for twelve seconds. On

(continues on next page)

their third attempt, they kept the plane in the air for fifty-nine seconds, traveling 852 feet in that time.

2   Only a few people witnessed the Wright brothers' flying experiments, which did not attract much publicity. As a result, many people who heard about the flight did not believe it had really happened. Inventors in Europe and the United States had been trying to build engine-powered flying machines for years. Who would believe that two bicycle mechanics from Dayton, Ohio, could succeed where so many others had failed?

3   The Wright brothers were not scientists, but they were mechanics. Observing that hawks controlled their flight by changing the position of their wings, Orville and Wilbur designed an aircraft with wings that could twist. These wings allowed the plane to turn, roll, and fly up and down. By 1905,

their airplanes could remain in the air for thirty minutes at a time. In 1909, the War Department contracted with the Wright brothers to produce the first U.S. Army planes.

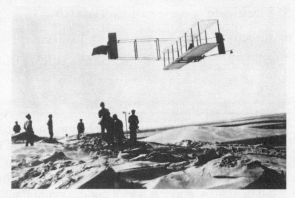

The Wright brothers take off.

CHECK YOUR COMPREHENSION

Mark each item true (T) or false (F).

_____ **1.** The Wright brothers flew their first airplane near Kitty Hawk, North Carolina.

_____ **2.** The Wright brothers' experiments in flying attracted a lot of public attention.

_____ **3.** The Wright brothers' observations of hawks helped them design their first aircraft.

_____ **4.** Most people who heard about the Wright brothers' flight believed it immediately.

_____ **5.** The Wright brothers were bicycle mechanics.

_____ **6.** The Wright brothers were the first people who tried to build an engine-powered aircraft.

BUILD YOUR READING SKILLS: Scanning

Scan Reading 2 to find answers to the questions. Work as quickly as you can.

1. How high did the Wright brothers' first aircraft travel? _____

2. When did the War Department contract the Wright brothers to produce planes for the army? _____

3. Where were the Wright brothers from? _____

4. How far did the Wright brothers travel on their third attempt at flying? _____

5. How long did the Wright brothers stay in the air on their first airplane trip? _____

6. When did the Wright brothers fly their first airplane? _____

BUILD YOUR READING SKILLS: Understanding How to Skim

Skimming is a reading technique you can use to learn the general idea of a passage. When you skim an article, you do not need to read every word because you are not looking for details.

Skim the newspaper articles on pages 106 and 107 about other important events in the early twentieth century. Try to find the general idea of each article. Then match the article with the appropriate headline from the list below. Write the correct headline on the line provided.

McKinley Shot

Art Show Shocks Crowds

Earthquake Shatters San Francisco

HOUDINI THRILLS AUDIENCE

Watch Out for the Model T

Peary Reaches North Pole

1. _____

PITTSBURGH, PENNSYLVANIA. Yesterday, 20,000 people crowded into the streets of Pittsburgh to see Harry Houdini wriggle out of a straightjacket while hanging upside down from a height of fifty feet. It seems that no jail cell, vault, straightjacket, packing case, or pair of handcuffs can contain the Great Houdini. Harry Houdini, one of America's greatest magicians, is famous for his abilities as an escape artist. Although Houdini has received challenges from countless people who believe they can securely bind, chain, handcuff, or imprison him, the great escape artist always proves each one wrong. Once again he has thrilled audiences with his amazing feats.

2. _____

Last week, after much anticipation, industrialist Henry Ford introduced his new car, the Model T, to the public. The Model T isn't Ford's first car. In 1893, after experimenting for several years, Henry Ford completed his first automobile. Then a few years later, in 1903, he established the Ford Motor Company, the leading manufacturer of cars. The Ford Motor Company has already produced a number of different models. So, what is it that makes the "T" so special? The answer is quite easy: The "T" is the first car on the market that the average person can afford to buy. It isn't very fancy, but it is reliable, cheap (only $850), and easy to fix. Henry Ford promises to look for ways to make the "T" even better and cheaper in the future

3. _____

SAN FRANCISCO. In the early morning hours of April 18, 1906, an earthquake shook the city and caused a fire that burned for three days, destroying almost all of San Francisco's downtown and much of the residential area. The earthquake was felt from southern Oregon to south of Los Angeles and inland as far as central Nevada. The earthquake lasted only a minute, but it caused the worst natural disaster in the nation's history. Over 490 city blocks and 25,000 buildings were destroyed. At least 700 people were killed, 500,000 lost their homes, and hundreds more were injured. The city's electric power lines went down, and gas and water mains were broken. Fires broke out and burned wildly for three days. Firefighters were unable to put the fire out because of damaged water mains. Damage estimates are estimated at more than $350,000,000.

4. _____

SEPTEMBER 14, 1901. President William Mckinley died today of complications from a gunshot wound. On September 6, President McKinley was greeting visitors at the Pan American Exposition in Buffalo, New York, when he was shot twice by anarchist Leon Czolgosz. The first bullet grazed his ribs, but the second bullet penetrated his abdomen. McKinley was rushed to a hospital where he underwent immediate surgery. Unfortunately, his condition worsened, and eight days after the shooting, the president died. Vice President Theodore Roosevelt was sworn into office as the new president this afternoon.

CULTURE
KERNEL

Teddy Bears are named after President Theodore "Teddy" Roosevelt. They were first introduced in 1902 and are still popular today.

5. _____

Audiences and critics alike were shocked at the opening of an art exhibit at New York's Armory on February 17, 1913. The international exhibit was the first major showing of modern art in the United States. It included cubist, expressionist, postimpressionist, and experimental works. Among the most talked about paintings was Marcel Duchamp's *Nude Descending a Staircase.*

6. _____

Explorer Robert Peary has become the first man to reach the North Pole. Peary led the expedition that consisted of his assistant Matthew A. Henson and four Inuit. They faced bad weather and shifting ice but finally reached their lifelong goal. He said he has "stood on the roof of the world." Peary is an American navy engineer who has spent his life trying to reach the Arctic. This was his third attempt. While the two earlier attempts did take Peary farther north than any previous explorers, he did not succeed in his main goal of reaching the North Pole.

CULTURE
KERNEL

In 1904, the ice cream cone was invented at the St. Louis World's Fair.

A new type of music called jazz was developed by black Americans at the beginning of the twentieth century. Today, jazz is still one of the most distinctly American art forms. The first jazz was played by black Americans in the dance halls of New Orleans in the early 1900s. In this article, you will learn how jazz moved in many new directions as it spread to different parts of the country. Today, jazz remains a popular musical style not only in the United States but also in countries all over the world.

BEFORE YOU READ

Discuss these questions with your classmates.

1. Do you like jazz? Who is your favorite jazz musician?
2. Have you ever been to a jazz club or a jazz concert?
3. Is jazz a popular musical style in your country?

The Jazz Sensation

1   The story of jazz is one of a musical form totally unlike any before it, even though jazz grew out of music that had existed for centuries. Jazz was not learned in schools. Many of its creators could not even read music. Early jazz often was not performed in formal concert halls with quiet, seated audiences like other music. Instead, jazz shows were outdoor events during which people marched, moved about, or sometimes rode in horse-drawn wagons.

2   The immigrants brought many musical traditions together in this country, but this alone did not account for the rise of jazz. Jazz needed the American environment and the experience of a special group of people—the slaves—to give it shape.

3   What made jazz different? It was experimental music that broke away from traditional musical forms. While it used the musical scales, melodies, and traditional instruments of the Europeans, it was not meant to be played as written. In fact, very little jazz was written. Jazz was a highly personal music that focused on individual interpretation and rhythm. The jazz musician had the freedom to vary the beat, the rhythm, and the volume as desired. This allowed the performer to compose and reshape the music according to his or her feelings. The freedom to change and experiment with the music while playing it—known as *improvisation*—is a main ingredient of jazz.

4   It took time for jazz to emerge as a distinct musical form, but this happened around the turn of the century. New Orleans had considerable influence on the development of jazz. It was a city full of music and good times influenced by several cultures—Spanish, French,

Jazz music has been popular for over 100 years.

Anglo-American, and African-American. Dances, parades, parties, shows, and banquets were common events that attracted and employed many musicians. Music could be heard all day long. French dance music, Spanish rhythms from the Caribbean, religious music, blues, slave work songs, and opera all mingled. This atmosphere created an ideal place for jazz to grow.

5   But the inspiration for jazz came primarily from the music, the feelings—in short, the history—of blacks in America. Black slaves were denied the chance to practice their African customs in America, and most were denied the opportunity to an education. So they found other ways of self-expression. Music was a large part of this, and it evolved into distinct styles. Blues and ragtime were the forerunners of jazz, and by the early 1900s, this new and recognizable style of music was being played by brass bands throughout the streets of New Orleans.

6   The popularity of jazz in New Orleans began to diminish in 1917. Many bars closed down. Musicians, out of work, began to leave the city. Some took Mississippi riverboats northbound. During the 1920s, Chicago became the new center for jazz. Other musicians traveled from California to New York, and even went on to Europe. As jazz spread, it gained popularity and developed new forms. Jazz musicians have continued to improvise, and because of this, jazz music has continued to change and evolve.

7   Jazz means different things to different people, and even the most enthusiastic jazz fans are sometimes unable to agree on what jazz is or how it should sound. But all agree that jazz is a truly American

CHECK YOUR COMPREHENSION

A. *Check (✓) the statements that are true about jazz, according to Reading 3.*

_____ **1.** Jazz is a truly American art form.

_____ **2.** Jazz is a formal style of music.

_____ **3.** Jazz musicians improvise their music.

_____ **4.** The inspiration for jazz came from the music of black slaves.

_____ **5.** Most jazz music is written down.

_____ **6.** Everybody agrees on what jazz is and how it should sound.

_____ **7.** Jazz music continues to change and evolve.

_____ **8.** Jazz music must be learned in schools.

B. *Answer the questions.*

1. What made jazz different from other forms of music?

_____

_____

2. Where and how was early jazz performed?

_____

_____

3. Where did the main inspiration for jazz come from?

_____

_____

4. Why has jazz continued to change and evolve?

_____

_____

EXPAND YOUR VOCABULARY

Complete each sentence with a word from the list. Change the form of the word if necessary.

rhythm	compose	volume
emerge	atmosphere	deny
diminish	evolve	enthusiastic

1. Women were _____ the right to vote until 1920.

2. Who _____ this beautiful piece of music?

3. Jazz _____ as a distinct musical form around 1900.

4. The _____ of the music in a jazz hall could be very loud.

5. The _____ in the room was warm and friendly.

6. The new teacher is an _____ jazz fan.

7. The _____ of African drum music is unique.

8. Jazz has continued to change and _____ over the years.

9. When the popularity of jazz began to _____, many musicians left the city.

BUILD YOUR READING SKILLS: Understanding References

Write the word or phrase that the word in bold type refers to.

1. What made jazz different? **It** was experimental music that broke from traditional musical forms.

   it = _____

2. The jazz musician had the freedom to vary the beat, the rhythm, and the volume as desired. **This** allowed the performer to compose and reshape the music according to his or her feelings.

   this = _____

3. Black slaves were denied the chance to practice their African customs in America, and most were denied the opportunity to an education. So **they** found other means of self-expression.

   they = _____

4. Music was a large part of this, and **it** evolved into distinct styles.

   it = _____

5. Musicians, out of work, began to leave the city. **Some** took Mississippi riverboats northbound.

   some = _____

6. Jazz musicians have continued to improvise, and because of **this**, jazz music has continued to change and evolve.

   this = _____

7. Jazz means different things to different people, and even the most enthusiastic jazz fans are sometimes unable to agree on what jazz is or how **it** should sound. But **all** agree that jazz is a truly American art form.

   it = _____

   all = _____

 LINKING PAST TO PRESENT Jazz is now 100 years old, and it remains a very popular kind of music. Today jazz musicians often make use of new technologies in the form of modern electronic instrumentation and recording devices. Jazz now incorporates Latin music, such as salsa and samba, and appeals to an international audience.

REACT AND RESPOND What type of music is your country famous for? How old is it and how has it changed over time?

WRITE ABOUT IT

On a separate piece of paper, write a paragraph about your favorite type of music.

READING 4 The Gilded Age

This article reviews a lot of the information you have studied. You will recognize many of the themes and terms in this article because you have read about them in other articles in this book. The author discusses what life in the United States was like during the years between the end of the Civil War and the beginning of World War I.

AS YOU READ

1. *The word* gild *means to cover with a thin layer of gold. As you read, think about why this time is referred to as the* Gilded Age.

2. *As you read, underline points of information that you are already familiar with.*

The Gilded Age
by Ellen Hardsog

1   The American way of life changed dramatically in the years between the end of the Civil War in 1865 and the outbreak of World War I in 1914. Increased industrial productivity and the consequent demand for factory-produced goods shifted the national economy from agriculture to industry and the population from farm to city. Everyone was eager to forget the shame of slavery and civil war and to explore new possibilities for prosperity. America was whole again, and there was no limit to the things Americans could do.

2   Mark Twain called these years "the Gilded Age" because of the way the rich tried to imitate the fancy dress, manners, homes, and entertainment of the British upper class. The families of bankers, lawyers, and factory owners enjoyed a fine way of life. The new industries made many millionaires, who drove ornate carriages, attended the opera and theater, and bought expensive toys for their children. They lived in huge mansions and took their vacations at the seashore in even bigger mansions, which they called "summer cottages."

3   Factory managers, small business owners, and gentlemen farmers also lived well during the Gilded Age. They became known as the middle class because they were neither rich nor poor. They lived in modest homes with new labor-saving inventions such as electric lights and telephones. Their families went to the

Huge mansions were built during the Gilded Age.

(continues on next page)

country for vacations. Many middle-class people traveled by train to visit the Philadelphia Centennial Exposition of 1876 and the Chicago World Columbian Exposition of 1893. The middle class enjoyed lectures, boating, roller-skating, and the new sport of baseball. Some of them later became wealthy.

4   If the age was gilded for the rich and middle class, it was something very different for the poor. Crowded into filthy tenements with several people to a room, the poor earned only a few pennies an hour but considered themselves lucky just to have jobs. Children as young as six years old worked in the factories to help support their families. They could attend shabby schools at night, but they learned little. Life was hard, and crime was a common alternative to working for low pay. The poor could not afford vacations.

5   Despite the hardships of poverty, there was always hope in the slums. Many of the poor were foreigners who had immigrated to the United States because they had heard that America was a land of golden opportunities. A few, such as manufacturer and philanthropist Andrew Carnegie, really did make a fortune, but for most factory workers, the dream lay in a better future for their children. Until that time should come, they banded together in protective ethnic neighborhoods, where they would not be persecuted for their different customs and languages.

6   For those who still wanted to farm, there was another kind of hope. The federal government offered land to people who would settle the West. As the growing cities swallowed up eastern farmland, wagon trains of farmers set out for the new territories. Some went for more room and others to prospect for gold. Of course, the land they took belonged to Indian tribes, and the U.S. Army was always trying, often

unsuccessfully, to defend the settlers from massacres. Those who survived had to battle the bad weather and insects that claimed their crops. More travelers came, however, encouraged by politicians who thought it was America's destiny to populate the land from sea to sea.

7   Politicians also caused trouble during the Gilded Age. They looked the other way while manufacturers fixed prices and exploited workers. Sometimes they joined businessmen in illegal moneymaking plans. Like the wealthy industrialists, their main interests were profit and power. The union of these two groups helped to widen the gap between rich and poor.

8   Investigative reporters known as *muckrakers* brought many crimes to public attention. They publicized corrupt business practices and the terrible lives of factory workers. Their reports led to improvements in areas such as wages, working environment, child labor laws, education, sanitation, and medical care.

9   When voters saw how many corrupt men were serving in public office, they began to look for more honest men to represent them. In time, the government became less influenced by business interests and began to break up the monopolies that major companies had built to control prices and markets. This action helped weaken industry's power over the people.

10   By the close of the Gilded Age, reformers had remedied many social injustices, and America was recovering from the growing pains of industrialization. Labor unions helped the working man, the automobile revolutionized travel, and the prairies were settled. The Gilded Age, though tarnished, brought the country to new heights of progress. America was firmly established as a world leader in technology, culture, and trade.

BUILD YOUR READING SKILLS: Recognizing Main Ideas

Write the number of the paragraph that ...

- _2_ **a.** describes the life of rich people during the Gilded Age.
- _5_ **b.** discusses ethnic neighborhoods where immigrants lived.
- _8_ **c.** tells what the muckrakers did.
- _6_ **d.** discusses farming in the West.
- _____ **e.** explains why the government took actions to break up the monopolies of major corporations.
- _3_ **f.** describes how the middle class lived during the Gilded Age.
- _1_ **g.** provides background information about the Gilded Age.
- _4_ **h.** describes the life of the poor during the Gilded Age.
- _____ **i.** makes concluding generalizations about the Gilded Age.
- _8_ **j.** discusses the corruption of politicians during the Gilded Age.

CHECK YOUR COMPREHENSION

*Mark each item true (**T**) or false (**F**).*

- _____ **1.** The gap between the rich and the poor became wider during the Gilded Age.

- _____ **2.** For the most part, politicians and industrialists fought against each other.

- _____ **3.** Farmers found hope in land offered by the government.

- _____ **4.** The middle class was made up of factory managers, small business owners, and gentlemen farmers.

- _____ **5.** Rich Americans did not approve of the lifestyle of the British upper class.

- _____ **6.** The middle class lived in fancy houses.

- _____ **7.** There were very few poor people during the Gilded Age.

- _____ **8.** The reports of the muckrakers led to social improvements.

- _____ **9.** The Gilded Age was a wonderful time for everyone who lived in the United States.

BUILD YOUR READING SKILLS: Understanding Details

Make a list of the details given in Reading 4 describing the lifestyle of each of these groups.

1. The Rich

_____

_____

_____

_____

2. The Middle Class

_____

_____

_____

_____

3. The Poor

_____

_____

_____

_____

EXPAND YOUR VOCABULARY

A. *Answer the questions.*

1. What word in paragraph 1 is a synonym of *resultant*? _____

2. What word in paragraph 2 is an antonym of *small*? _____

3. What word in paragraph 2 is an antonym of *plain*? _____

4. What word in paragraph 2 means *to copy*? _____

5. What word in paragraph 3 means *not large in size or value*?

   _____

6. What words in paragraph 3 are examples of *labor-saving inventions*?

   _____

7. What word in paragraph 4 means *dirty*? _____

8. What word in paragraph 4 means *run-down*? _____

CULTURE
KERNEL

In 1903, the first movie with a story was made. It was called **The Great Train Robbery.**

B. *Complete each sentence with the correct form of a word from the list.*

1. produce, productivity, producer, product, production, productive

    a. It was a long and _____ meeting.

    b. My uncle's factory _____ shoes.

    c. The _____ of iron decreased in the last decade.

    d. The United States is one of the biggest _____ of steel in the world.

    e. The company's _____ include televisions and VCRs.

    f. Computers have helped to increase _____ in offices around the country.

2. economy, economic, economical, economics, economize

    a. To save money and energy, you should _____ on gasoline.

    b. A small car is more _____ than a large one.

    c. My _____ course is very difficult.

    d. The country is in a bad _____ condition.

    e. The new president promised to improve the state of the _____ .

3. prosper, prosperity, prosperous

    a. There was a time of _____ after the war ended.

    b. Farmers _____ when good weather allows them to grow healthy crops.

    c. We became more _____ as our business grew.

4. manager, manage, management, managerial, manageable

    a. She _____ her money very well.

    b. I'm looking for a _____ position in the company.

    c. The _____ is negotiating with the union.

    d. This food is terrible; I'm going to complain to the _____ of the restaurant.

    e. There is a lot of work to do, but it's _____ .

5. invent, invention, inventive, inventor

    a. The electric lightbulb is a wonderful _____ .

    b. Thomas Edison _____ the electric lightbulb.

    c. Thomas Edison was the _____ of the electric lightbulb.

    d. Thomas Edison was an _____ person.

6. protect, protection, protector, protective

    a. My mother is very _____ of her children.

    b. Sunscreen offers _____ from the harmful rays of the sun.

    c. I _____ my skin with sunscreen when I go to the beach.

    d. A parent is a child's _____.

7. industrialize, industrialist, industry, industrious, industrial

    a. He is very _____ and started his own business.

    b. _____ production is rising every year.

    c. Building factories is a key step in _____ a country's economy.

    d. The U.S. automobile _____ is centered in Detroit, Michigan.

    e. An owner of a large factory is an _____.

8. corrupt, corruption, corruptible

    a. The muckrakers wanted to expose _____ in business and politics.

    b. The _____ police officer was accepting bribes from criminals.

    c. He was sent to jail for trying to _____ a police officer.

WRITE ABOUT IT

Use your lists from page 116 as a guide to write a paragraph on a separate piece of paper describing the differences in lifestyles among the rich, the middle class, and the poor during the Gilded Age. Include information about housing, vacations, entertainment, and transportation.

Some of the problems of the Gilded Age are still problems today. For example, a huge gap still exists between the rich and the poor. Many people, especially immigrants and minorities, still live in poor conditions. Their housing is often unsafe and unhealthy.

REACT AND RESPOND Is there a big gap between the rich and the poor in your country? If so, what kinds of problems does this gap cause?

HISTORY MAKER: Jane Addams

Carefully read the following list of facts about Jane Addams, an important reformer in the Progressive movement. Then choose the information you want from the list to write a paragraph about her on a separate piece of paper. Be sure to begin your paragraph with a topic sentence that states the main idea. Include transition words to guide the reader from one point to the next.

Jane Addams, social reformer

- worked to improve lives of the poor
- born in Cedarville, Illinois, in 1869
- educated at Rockford Female Seminary and Women's Medical College and in Europe
- founded Hull House, a community center in Chicago
- raised money from wealthy to help the poor
- helped pass a factory inspection law and establish a juvenile court
- lobbied for workmen's compensation and Prohibition
- helped pass laws forbidding children under age fourteen to work
- was active in women's issues
- believed that women could shape their own destinies
- worked for women's right to vote
- was strongly against World War I
- founded Women's International League for Peace and Freedom in 1915 and served as president, 1919–1929
- was first American woman recipient of Nobel Peace Prize in 1931
- died in 1935

Exchange paragraphs with a partner. Read your partner's paragraph and check it for correct grammar, punctuation, and capitalization.

Read the passage about the origins of baseball and complete the exercise that follows.

Baseball

1   The game of baseball is based on a British game called rounders, **which** was popular in England in the 1600s. The colonists brought **it** with them to the New World. Over the course of time, Americans slowly changed rounders into the game we know as baseball. In 1845, Alexander Cartwright wrote the first set of rules for baseball. The **game** started in the eastern United States. The Civil War helped **it** spread throughout the country. Soldiers from both the North and the South taught it to other soldiers. **They** took it home with them after the war and taught it to their friends. In 1869, the Cincinnati Red Stockings became the first team to be paid to play baseball. This was the beginning of professional baseball. By 1876, there were eight professional teams. **They** called themselves the National League. In 1900, eight other teams formed the American League. During the early 1900s, the game of baseball was so popular in the United States that **it** became known as the national pastime. Major league baseball continues to enjoy widespread popularity.

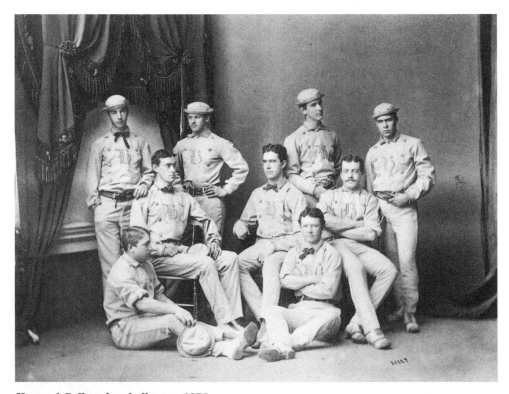

Harvard College baseball team, 1875

Look back at the passage. Write the word or phrase that the words in bold type refer to.

1. which = _____

2. it = _____

3. game = _____

4. it = _____

5. They = _____

6. They = _____

7. it = _____

PUT IT TOGETHER

Discuss the questions.

1. American culture can be described as informal. For example, Americans often address older people by their first names, and many Americans dress casually even for work. Is your culture more formal or informal? Give specific examples to support your answer.

2. Working hard is an important value in the United States. But Americans also put a lot of emphasis on having fun and being entertained. How much emphasis does your culture put on having fun? What are the most popular forms of entertainment in your country?

3. American society is often characterized as being socially mobile. A person's place in society is not completely determined by his or her birth. What are the advantages of a being a member of a socially mobile society? Is society in your country socially mobile? How much is your place in society determined by birth?

CHAPTER 6

PROSPERITY AND DEPRESSION

The 1920s and 1930s

In this chapter, you will learn about the prosperity and good times in the United States during the 1920s and the Depression and hard times during the 1930s.

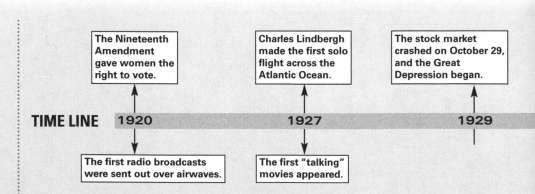

MAKE A CONNECTION

What was happening in your country between 1920 and 1939?

TIME LINE

	The Nineteenth Amendment gave women the right to vote.		Charles Lindbergh made the first solo flight across the Atlantic Ocean.		The stock market crashed on October 29, and the Great Depression began.
	1920		**1927**		**1929**
	The first radio broadcasts were sent out over airwaves.		The first "talking" movies appeared.		

The United States in the 1920s and 1930s

The 1920s and 1930s were about as different as two decades in the same country could be.

Postwar Prosperity

After World War I, Americans were ready to celebrate. It was a time of prosperity for many, but not all, people. During this time, American society changed in many ways. The automobile allowed people to move out of cities and into suburbs. Many women began going to college, working outside the home, and getting married later. The literature, art, fashions, and music of the 1920s reflected the young and the fun-loving spirit of the times. Business boomed, and advertisements encouraged people to spend their money on "luxury" items such as cars, refrigerators, and washing machines.

During World War I, Congress had passed the Eighteenth Amendment, making the manufacture and sale of alcohol illegal. This law, however, was impossible to enforce during the fun-loving times of the 1920s, and alcohol remained easy to get. Serious problems resulted: Gangsters found that providing illegal alcohol made them a lot of money, and they fought violently for control of their new business. Congress repealed, or canceled, the Eighteenth Amendment in 1933.

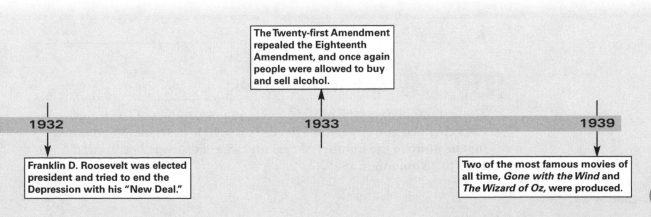

The Twenty-first Amendment repealed the Eighteenth Amendment, and once again people were allowed to buy and sell alcohol.

1932 **1933** **1939**

Franklin D. Roosevelt was elected president and tried to end the Depression with his "New Deal."

Two of the most famous movies of all time, *Gone with the Wind* and *The Wizard of Oz,* were produced.

The Great Depression

Most people thought the prosperity of the 1920s would never end. But in October 1929, the stock market crashed and upset the entire economy. This was the beginning of the Great Depression, the worst economic period in American history. Thousands of businesses and banks closed, and millions of people lost money. That year, more than 12 million people lost their jobs. In 1932, Franklin Delano Roosevelt was elected president. He gave hope to millions of suffering Americans by starting programs that created jobs and helped the poor.

Growth of Popular Entertainment

During the Depression, people tried to escape from their problems by listening to the radio and going to the movies. Radio was the cheapest form of entertainment, and during the 1930s, the number of radios went from 13 million to 27 million. Movies were the most popular type of entertainment. Because ticket prices were so cheap, most Americans were able to go to the movies at least once a week and forget their hard times, at least for a short while.

CULTURE KERNEL

In 1921, the first Miss America contest was held.

Answer the questions.

1. What were some changes that took place in the United States during the 1920s?

    a. _____

    b. _____

    c. _____

    d. _____

2. What were some effects of the Depression on American society?

    a. _____

    b. _____

    c. _____

3. How did people entertain themselves during the Depression?

    a. _____

    b. _____

READING 1   America on Wheels

The automobile was the most important new product of the times. Cars changed how Americans lived. This article describes the reasons for the jump in the number of cars on U.S. roads from 7 million in 1919 to 23 million in 1929.

BUILD YOUR READING SKILLS: Previewing

Preview the article by following these steps.

1. Look at the title of the article and write it on the line. What do you think this article will be about?

   _____

   _____

2. Read the subtitle and write it on the line. What do you think the main idea of this article might be?

   _____

   _____

3. Write the headings on the lines and predict what each section will be about.

   a. _____

   _____

   b. _____

   _____

   c. _____

   _____

   d. _____

   _____

4. Read the first and last paragraphs of the article to get a general overview of the whole article.

5. This article contains one picture. Why do you think this picture was included?

6. Read the first sentence of each paragraph to understand the main idea of the paragraph.

7. Now read the article all the way through. Do not stop reading to look up words in the dictionary and do not worry about parts that you do not understand. The purpose of the first reading is simply to give you a general sense of the article and to prepare you for a more careful reading.

America on Wheels

by Sean McCollum

Americans Exchanged Horses for Horsepower and Roared into the Roaring Twenties

1   The 1920s were a decade of dramatic change in American society. Everything, from work to sexual morality, seemed to be changing quickly. Country folk were leaving their farms for factory jobs in cities. U.S. soldiers returned from Europe, still young but now worldly wise, to share their experiences of the First World War. Women—full-fledged voters as of 1920—could vote and became a political force. But exciting as these changes were, they weren't the most important force shaping America.

2   The 1920s were the decade of the automobile. From 1919 to 1929, the number of cars on the road more than tripled, from 6.8 million to 23.1 million. The car went from being a rich person's toy to everyone's necessity and in the process changed life for an entire generation. The speed and range of cars changed where people lived and vacationed. The roads they needed changed the landscape around them. The factories needed to build them changed the way people worked. The car—and its backseat—even changed the way young people dated.

HENRY'S MODEL T

3   The "horseless carriage" had been around since the late 1800s. But it took Henry Ford to find a way to make cars affordable for most Americans. Born a Michigan farm boy, Ford (1863–1947) was a brilliant inventor. But it was his vision of mass production that qualified him as a genius.

THE NEW CRAZE OF THE 1920S

4   In 1906, Ford declared, "The automobile of the future must be . . . low enough in price to ensure sales for the enormously increased output. The car of the future, 'car for the people,' the car that any man can own who can afford a horse and carriage, is coming sooner than most people expect."

Model T Fords come off the assembly line.

5   It came in 1913. That year, Ford opened a new plant in Highland Park, Michigan. There, Ford and his engineers adapted an "assembly-line" process for building the Model T Ford.

6   The assembly line revolutionized the way manufactured products were made. In earlier manufacturing, workers performed many tasks, often building an entire product from start to finish. But on an assembly line, workers stood in one place while the car and necessary parts came to them. Each worker then performed the same tasks over and over. The tasks were about as exciting as washing dishes, but they greatly speeded up the building process. The time it took to build the Model T dropped from 12½ hours to 1 hour and 33 minutes.

7   More efficient production meant reduced costs. Lower prices meant more Americans could afford to jump behind the wheel. Americans bought the Model T in record numbers, in the process making Ford a millionaire.

8   The "Tin Lizzie," as the Model T was nicknamed, was the McDonald's hamburger of automobiles. More than 15 million Model T's rolled off assembly lines between 1908 and 1927. Almost overnight, automobile manufacturing became the largest industry in the United States.

ON THE ROAD

9   By 1927, one in five Americans owned a car, a figure eight times higher than in any other country. The car appealed to Americans' restless natures. Many were even willing to cut back on necessities. When a farmer's wife was asked why she had a car but no bathtub, she answered, "Well, you can't get to town in a bathtub."

10   Never had so many people been so mobile. Cars meant that workers could live farther from their jobs, which fueled the growth of city suburbs.

11   The car also gave rise to a new fad—auto camping. Families could put a tent and some cans of food in the car and go exploring. They saw more of their country, and fellow Americans, than had ever been possible before. "For the first time in history," wrote a popular newspaper columnist, C. P. Russell, in 1925, "the common, ordinary folks of the North and South are meeting one another on a really large scale, mostly by means of the national chariot—the Ford car."

12   Roadside industries were started to serve the new "autoists." By the end of the decade, there were more than 120,000 gas stations nationwide. Cheap hotels, called motels, lined major routes. Small towns set up free campgrounds for tourists.

13   The car might have given common people the means of moving, but the roads were still dangerous. A road system barely existed and basically had to be built from scratch. Only about 1 percent of country roads in 1920 were paved. The increasing number of auto owners put pressure on the government to build better and safer roads. By the end of the 1920s, 10,000 miles of roads were being built a year.

14   Road signs and maps also were new concepts. Their short supply provided plenty of material for jokes in popular magazine and radio shows of the day:

(continues on next page)

Driver: Do you know which road goes to Chicago?

Country boy: No.

Driver: Do you know which road goes to Joliet?

Country boy: No.

Driver: You don't know anything, do you?

Country boy: Yes, sir. I know I'm not lost.

AUTO-MORALITY

15   At the same time, the car was blamed for many social ills. Critics blamed it for causing a decline in church attendance (too many Sunday drives), for increasing crime (too many quick getaways), and for corrupting the nation's youth (too much kissing in the backseat).

16   Not surprisingly, kids quickly discovered the advantages of going out on auto dates. Before the car, it was tough for a young couple to get out from under the watchful eyes of parents. Now, though, kids could hop in the car and drive to a dance in a distant town. They could also "run out of gas" on a lonely country road on the way home.

17   But love it or hate it, the car shook, rattled, rolled, and changed American society. The humorist Will Rogers said it best at the time. "Good luck, Mr. Ford. It will take a hundred years to tell whether you have helped us or hurt us, but you certainly didn't leave us like you found us."

**CULTURE
KERNEL**

In 1913, Ford's assembly line built 260,720 cars. The other 299 car makers built a combined total of 280,770 cars.[1]

CHECK YOUR COMPREHENSION

A. *Circle the letter of the choice that best completes each sentence.*

1. According to the article, the most important force shaping American society in the 1920s was _____.
   - **a.** politics
   - **b.** the automobile
   - **c.** sexual morality
   - **d.** factory jobs

2. From 1919 to 1929, the number of cars on the roads _____.
   - **a.** significantly increased
   - **b.** more than tripled
   - **c.** went from about 7 million to 23 million
   - **d.** all of the above

3. The availability of cars changed all of the following except _____.
   - **a.** where people lived and vacationed
   - **b.** the way young people dated
   - **c.** factory workers' pay
   - **d.** the roads and landscapes

---

[1]"Seeing the Century," *American Heritage,* December 1999: 36.

4. The assembly-line process _____.
   (a.) revolutionized the way cars were made
   b. caused the price of cars to increase
   c. made factory work more interesting
   d. increased the amount of time it took to produce a car

5. Cars fueled the growth of suburbs because _____.
   a. factories moved out of the cities
   b. people could move farther from their jobs
   c. roadside industries became popular
   d. labor in the suburbs was cheaper

6. In 1920, most roads in the United States were _____.
   a. paved and safe
   b. superhighways
   (c.) unpaved and dangerous
   d. build by the government

7. Cars were blamed for all of the following social problems except
_____.
   a. declining church attendance
   b. increasing the amount of crime
   c. corrupting youth
   (d.) lowering the educational standards

B. *Mark each item true (**T**) or false (**F**).*

  _T_ **1.** By 1927, auto manufacturing was the largest industry in the
         United States.

  _T_ **2.** American society experienced great social change in the 1920s.

  _F_ **3.** The first Model T was built in the late 1800s.

  _T_ **4.** The Model T was nicknamed the "Tin Lizzie."

  _F_ **5.** More than 50 percent of Americans owned cars in 1927.

  _T_ **6.** Auto camping became a popular activity in the 1920s.

  _F_ **7.** Henry Ford believed automobiles should be owned only by rich
         people.

  _F_ **8.** Workers on an assembly line perform many different tasks.

In 1932, Amelia Earhart became the first woman to make a solo flight across the Atlantic Ocean.

BUILD YOUR READING SKILLS: Examining Meaning

*Read each sentence. Then read the five statements that follow it. Based on information in the original sentence, make a judgment about each statement. If it is true, write a **T** on the line. If it is false, write an **F**. If there is not enough information in the original sentence to make a judgment, write **?***

1. Almost overnight, automobile manufacturing became the largest industry in the United States.

   _T_ a. Automobile manufacturing quickly became a large industry.

   _F_ b. Automobile manufacturing had always been a large industry in the United States.

   _F_ c. Automobile manufacturing became a large industry in the middle of the night.

   _T_ d. Cotton was the biggest industry in the United States before automobiles were invented.

   _F_ e. In the past, automobile manufacturing had not been a large industry.

2. The tasks were about as exciting as washing dishes, but they greatly speeded up the building process.

   _F_ a. Washing dishes is an exciting task.

   _T_ b. The tasks were boring.

   _F_ c. Washing dishes greatly speeded up the building process.

   _?_ d. The tasks were very exciting.

   _T_ e. The tasks decreased the time involved in the building process.

3. Women—full-fledged voters as of 1920—became a political force.

   _T_ a. Women were not a strong political force before 1920.

   _F_ b. Women voted regularly before 1920.

   _T_ c. Having the right to vote made women a political force.

   _?_ d. Eighty percent of women voted in political elections after 1920.

   _T_ e. Women gained the right to vote in 1920.

4. Americans bought the Model T in record numbers, in the process making Ford a millionaire.

   _?_ a. Americans recorded the number of cars they bought.

   _T_ b. Ford became rich because so many Americans bought Model Ts.

   _F_ c. Few Americans bought the Model T Fords.

   _?_ d. Eight million Americans bought Model T Fords.

   _?_ e. Ford was born into a wealthy family.

5. Never had so many people been so mobile.

   _F_   **a.** Few people were mobile.

   _I_   **b.** Many people were mobile.

   _I_   **c.** Fewer people were mobile in the past.

   _F_   **d.** Everyone became mobile.

   _I_   **e.** Some people never became mobile.

6. A road system barely existed and basically had to be built from scratch.

   _F_   **a.** The roads were badly scratched.

   _I_   **b.** There was almost no road system.

   _F_   **c.** There was already an extensive road system.

   _I_   **d.** The government wanted to build the road system.

   _I_   **e.** A road system needed to be built.

7. Not surprisingly, kids quickly discovered the advantages of going out on auto dates.

   _I_   **a.** Kids realized the advantages of going out on auto dates.

   _?_   **b.** Kids were not surprised about the advantages of auto dating.

   _?_   **c.** Adults disapproved of auto dating.

   _F_   **d.** All kids enjoyed going out on auto dates.

   _F_   **e.** It took kids a surprisingly long time to discover the advantages of auto dating.

EXPAND YOUR VOCABULARY

Circle the two words in each row that are closest in meaning.

1. entire	enjoy	whole	part
2. adaptable	affordable	inexpensive	expensive
3. brilliant	bitter	dull	smart
4. fight	revolutionize	change	increase
5. job	trash	task	think
6. tired	restless	anxious	happy
7. dishonest	helpful	depressed	corrupt

WRITE ABOUT IT

Some people love to drive and love the freedom that owning a car gives them. Other people view cars as an expensive annoyance, another machine that is always breaking. How do you feel about cars? On a separate piece of paper, write a paragraph explaining your thoughts.

CULTURE KERNEL

By 1930, thirty-eight airlines were flying passengers all over the U.S. and to other countries.

LINKING PAST TO PRESENT The president of Michigan Savings Bank once told Henry Ford, "The auto is only a fad!" In 1900, there were 8,000 automobiles in the United States. In 2000, there were more than 130 million. The auto wasn't a fad; it was here to stay. In fact, today, many American households have two or more cars.

REACT AND RESPOND Is it common for people in your country to own more than one car? Why or why not?

READING 2 **The Harlem Renaissance**

Transportation wasn't the only thing being revolutionized in the 1920s. The literature, art, and music of the 1920s also underwent changes. In this article, you will read about an African-American literary, musical, and artistic movement of the 1920s that reflected the changing times. On page 135, you will read a poem by Langston Hughes, one of the best-known writers of the Harlem Renaissance.

The Harlem Renaissance

1   Come with us. It is a hot summer night in Harlem, New York, 1926. Well-dressed people from downtown Manhattan are enthusiastically traveling by subway to this neighborhood. Others who live in the area eagerly leave their small apartments. The music of the blues and jazz can be heard coming from the nightclubs.

2   In the 1920s and early 1930s, Harlem was the largest black urban community in the country. Many African Americans had moved there from the South in the two decades since 1900. Harlem was a community of families, homes, and businesses. It also was the spiritual center of the Harlem Renaissance, a 1920s artistic movement made up of black writers, poets,

dancers, singers, actors, composers, and painters. A *renaissance* is a rebirth or rediscovery and is often a time when much artistic activity takes place. Black artists in the 1920s were interested not only in rediscovering their African roots and culture but also in understanding their place in American society.

3   The times—the Roaring Twenties—played a big role in giving these artists the opportunity to express their black experiences. World War I had just ended; times were better economically for the black middle class; and people everywhere got rid of old ideas and accepted new ones. Black artists were eager to be heard, and many people listened.

4   The artists of the Harlem Renaissance were not a formal, organized group. They did not attend scheduled weekly meetings or share a common political or philosophical belief. It was this growing black city, Harlem, and their common cultural experience that brought them together. Most of these artists lived in Harlem and saw each other on the streets, in the library, and at parties. Many were friends. Some wealthy white people helped get African-American art published, performed, and exhibited.

5   In the 1930s, the economy collapsed and hurt the Harlem Renaissance. Money was no longer available to support the artists, and Harlem lost its focus as the center of the movement. But the creativity of the artists did not die. The spirit of the renaissance and the art it produced still enrich those who enjoy it and inspire new artists, both black and white.

Harlem, New York, in the 1920s—the birthplace of the Harlem Renaissance

CHECK YOUR COMPREHENSION

*Mark each item true (**T**) or false (**F**).*

_____ **1.** Harlem was the largest black urban community in the United States in the 1920s and 1930s.

_____ **2.** Black artists in the 1920s were only interested in understanding their place in American society.

_____ **3.** The economic situation of middle-class blacks improved after World War I.

_____ **4.** The artists of the Harlem Renaissance organized a formal group.

_____ **5.** The spirit of the Harlem Renaissance has not died out.

BUILD YOUR READING SKILLS: Using Context to Understand Vocabulary

Using clues such as punctuation, grammar, and the general meaning of the sentence, try to figure out the meaning of the words in bold type. Write an approximate definition or synonym of the word. Do not use your dictionary.

1. Harlem was a **community** of families, homes, and businesses.

   _____

2. A *renaissance* is a rebirth or rediscovery and is often a time when much artistic activity takes place.

   _____

3. World War I had just ended; times were better economically for the black middle class; and people everywhere **got rid** of old ideas and accepted new ones.

   _____

4. Black artists were **eager** to be heard, and many people listened.

   _____

5. The spirit of the renaissance and the art it produced still **enrich** those who enjoy it and inspire new artists, both black and white.

   _____

BUILD YOUR READING SKILLS: Summarizing

Summarizing is a good way to help you understand an article and identify the author's main ideas. When you summarize, you should reduce the article to its main points in several clear sentences. When you write a summary, you should think about *who*, *what*, *when*, *where*, and *why*.

Read these three summaries of Reading 2 and answer the questions.

1   The Harlem Renaissance was a movement in the 1920s made up of black writers, poets, musicians, and artists who wanted to rediscover their African roots and understand their place in American society. Although they were not an organized group, many were friends who lived in Harlem. During the Harlem Renaissance, African-American art was widely published, performed, and exhibited, often with help from wealthy white people. When the economy collapsed in the 1930s, the Harlem Renaissance began to fade, but its spirit did not die and the art that was produced during this time continues to be an inspiration to artists today.

2   After World War I, the economy improved and America entered the Roaring Twenties. Many people, including black artists, were caught up in the excitement of the times and wanted their ideas to be heard. Some of these artists formed a movement called the Harlem Renaissance. Although the movement was important, it was not a formal group with a specific set of beliefs. Many of the artists lived in Harlem, which was the largest black community in the United States. Black artists in the Harlem Renaissance often met on the street, in the library, or at bars.

3   The Harlem Renaissance was the most important artistic movement of the 1920s. During this time, black writers, poets, dancers, composers, and painters produced better work than they ever had before. Unfortunately, the collapse of the economy in the 1930s put an end to the Harlem Renaissance.

1. Which paragraph gives too much personal opinion and not enough facts?

_____

2. Which paragraph gives unimportant details and omits some of the important points from the original article? _____

3. Which paragraph provides the best summary of the original article?

_____

Langston Hughes was one of the most important artists of the Harlem Renaissance. He is best remembered for his poems that deal with the concerns of African Americans. Read this poem by Langston Hughes and complete the exercises.

DREAM DEFERRED

What happens to a dream deferred?
Does it dry up
Like a raisin in the sun?
Or fester like a sore—
And then run?
Does it stink like rotten meat?
Or crust and sugar over—
like a syrupy sweet?
Maybe it just sags
like a heavy load.
Or does it explode?

BUILD YOUR SKILLS: Understanding Similes

A *simile* is an expression in which you compare two different things using the words *like* or *as*. Similes are used to create a picture in the reader's mind.

Example: She sings *like a bird*.

Her hair is *as black as night*.

Hughes used a series of similes to express his ideas about a deferred dream. Go back to the poem and underline the five similes.

WRITE ABOUT IT

Think about images of a dream fulfilled. What would you compare a dream fulfilled to? Write five similes that express your idea of a dream fulfilled.

1. A dream fulfilled is like _____.

2. A dream fulfilled is like _____.

3. A dream fulfilled is like _____.

4. A dream fulfilled is like _____.

5. A dream fulfilled is like _____.

TALK ABOUT IT

In your opinion, what happens to a dream if it is deferred?

CULTURE KERNEL

Boxing became a popular spectator sport during the 1930s and 1940s.

READING 3 Rock Bottom

Although it seemed to many that the prosperity of the 1920s would continue for years, in 1929, the stock market crashed and upset the whole economy. The Great Depression that followed lasted more than a decade. Hundreds of thousands of Americans lost their jobs, businesses failed, and financial institutions closed. The Great Depression did not end until after the United States entered World War II in 1941. In this article, you will read about the effects of the Depression on one man's family.

Rock Bottom
by Ellen Whitford

The 1930s Were the Toughest Economic Times in U.S. History. One Man Remembers What It Was Like.

People wait in line for food during the Great Depression.

1   Terry Clipper was fourteen years old when his parents lost their jobs, and their home, in the Great Depression. Today, Clipper is in his seventies. But his memories of the Depression era are still keen.

2   It was in 1931, two years after the collapse of the U.S. economy began, that Terry's family lost everything—their land, their livestock, and their home. His father could no longer pay the taxes he owed on the family's central Oklahoma farm. Nor could he repay the money he had borrowed to purchase cattle. So a local bank seized the Clippers' family farm.

3   "My mother and father were strong people," Clipper, who now lives in California, says. "But that ruined them. All they had were seven hungry children. No

(continues on next page)

home. No hope. No future. No nothing. I remember how they cried."

4   Terry, the oldest son, dropped out of school that year, after completing ninth grade. His family needed whatever he could earn.

5   "We didn't have money for anything—not for clothes, or shoes, or a bar of candy," Clipper says. "I remember many other people in our town, people who didn't have anything to eat or anywhere to live."

6   The Depression was a time of great fear and widespread poverty throughout America. The crisis began in October 1929, during the administration of President Herbert Hoover, when the stock market collapsed. By 1932, more than 100,000 businesses had failed and a quarter of the nation's work force—nearly 15 million people—had no jobs.

7   Millions of hungry citizens stood in breadlines. Some looked in garbage dumps for bones or rotting food. In rural areas, one historian writes, "Millions stayed alive by living like animals," eating weeds and roots. Others starved.

8   Homelessness was also a problem. The U.S. Census Bureau says that more than 1 million Americans became homeless in 1933. Other estimates set the number even higher—between 2 million and 5 million.

9   Thousands of citizens—desperate for work—took to the road as migrants. In the cities, families lived in corridors, abandoned construction sites, and shacks built of cardboard, scrap lumber, and other discarded materials. Shantytowns sprang up across the country, dubbed "Hoovervilles," after the president who was considered their "architect." Hundreds of people were driven to commit suicide, and many more considered it.

THE "NEW DEAL"

10   A new president, Franklin D. Roosevelt, responded to the emergency by trying to improve the nation's spirits. "The only thing we have to fear is fear itself," Roosevelt told the American people in a speech. After taking office, he began a revolutionary plan to break the Depression. He created a series of federally sponsored programs and agencies that were referred to collectively as the "New Deal." Its programs put millions of Americans to work.

11   Terry's father was employed by a program called the Works Progress Administration (WPA). The WPA spent $11 billion to provide jobs for 8.5 million people. It built or improved more than 651,000 miles of roads and streets, 124,000 bridges, 125,000 government buildings, 8,000 parks, and 850 airports. It also hired nearly 5,000 artists, who gave free art lessons and painted murals in post offices and other public buildings.

12   Terry found work with still another New Deal program—the Civilian Conservation Corps (CCC). The CCC put young, single men to work building roads, planting trees, constructing fences, and installing telephone lines. Terry lived in government camps, where he received food, clothes, and $30 a month. He sent $25 of that money home to his family to help pay for food, clothes, and rent.

13   "If it hadn't been for President Roosevelt and those programs," Clipper now says, "I don't know what my family would have done."

DEPRESSION PERSISTS

14   Yet neither Terry's family, nor millions like them, recovered completely from the Depression. In 1937, President Roosevelt said he still saw "one-third of [the] nation ill-housed, ill-clad, and ill-nourished." And in 1939, ten years after the Depression began, more than 9 million people remained unemployed, and several million people were still homeless.

15   Those figures began decreasing only after the United States entered World War II in December 1941. The demand for weapons and other supplies provided countless jobs. Meanwhile, Terry and other young men went off to fight in the war. After the war, U.S. soldiers came back to a booming economy. Aided by low-interest government loans, they and millions of other Americans could finally afford homes of their own. The Great Depression was over—but their memories of it would never fade.

BUILD YOUR READING SKILLS: Recognizing Main Ideas

Write the number of the paragraph(s) that . . .

_____ **a.** explains the effects of World War II on the American economy.

_____ **b.** discusses Roosevelt's plan to end the Depression.

_____ **c.** describes what happened to the Clipper family as a result of the Depression.

_____ **d.** gives statistics about business failures and unemployment.

_____ **e.** describes the terrible living conditions of some people during the Depression.

_____ **f.** describes what the Works Progress Administration did.

CHECK YOUR COMPREHENSION

Circle the letter of the choice that best completes each sentence.

1. The Works Progress Administration (WPA) _____.
   a. provided jobs for millions of people
   b. was a New Deal program
   c. hired artists
   d. all of the above

2. The Depression caused all of the following except _____.
   a. homelessness   **c.** industrialization
   b. unemployment   **d.** hunger

3. Terry Clipper dropped out of school because _____.
   a. he was a poor student
   b. he needed to work
   c. many high schools closed
   d. he wanted to move to California

4. When the stock market collapsed, _____.
    a. businesses and banks closed   **c.** the economy boomed
    b. employment rose   **d.** car sales increased

5. Roosevelt's federally sponsored programs and agencies were called
_____.
    a. shantytowns   **c.** the New Deal
    b. Hoovervilles   **d.** the Great Depression

6. Ten years after the Depression began, _____.
    a. almost all Americans were back to work
    b. 9 million people were still unemployed
    c. homelessness was no longer a problem
    d. Roosevelt started the WPA and the CCC

BUILD YOUR READING SKILLS: Understanding References

Write the word or phrase that the word in bold type refers to.

1. Terry, the oldest son, dropped out of school that year, after completing ninth grade. **His** family needed whatever he could earn.

    his = _____

2. Millions of hungry citizens stood in breadlines. **Some** looked in garbage dumps for bones or rotting food.

    some = _____

3. Hundreds of people were driven to commit suicide, and many more considered **it**.

    it = _____

4. After the war, U.S. soldiers came back to a booming economy. Aided by low-interest government loans, **they** and millions of other Americans could finally afford homes of their own.

    they = _____

5. In 1937, President Roosevelt said **he** still saw "one-third of [the] nation ill-housed, ill-clad, and ill-nourished."

    he = _____

EXPAND YOUR VOCABULARY

A. *Match each word or phrase with its synonym.*

_____ 1. keen   a. quit

_____ 2. collapse   b. many

_____ 3. seized   c. sharp

_____ 4. drop out   d. took

_____ 5. booming   e. thriving

_____ 6. countless   f. fall

B. *Complete each sentence with the correct form of a word from the list.*

1. employ, employable, employee, employer, employment

   a. My _____ is IBM.

   b. When he graduates, he'll be looking for _____ in California.

   c. To be _____, I need good skills.

   d. She works for the government. She is a government _____.

   e. That factory used to _____ more than 2,000 people.

2. begin, beginner, beginning

   a. He _____ his career with this company five years ago.

   b. The placement test is given at the _____ of the semester.

   c. This is the first time she has ever played golf. She is a
   _____.

3. desperate, desperately, desperation

   a. The drowning man grabbed his friend in _____.

   b. After he graduated, he was _____ to find a job.

   c. He wanted _____ to find a good job.

4. pay, payable, payment

   a. She told me to make the check _____ to ESL Inc.

   b. I think we will receive _____ for our work next week.

   c. Do you think we _____ too much money for our car?

5. construct, construction, constructive

   a. They are _____ another runway at the airport.

   b. My boss is good at giving me _____ ideas to help me solve problems.

   c. Several new buildings are under _____ downtown.

LINKING PAST TO PRESENT While the Depression was going on around them, Americans turned to entertainment for escape. "America went mad for movies. In 1930, in a country of 130 million people, movie attendance hit 90 million a week. The big screen created the strongest popular culture since Charles Dickens and defined for the world a characteristic American style—friendly, open, and optimistic."[2]

REACT AND RESPOND Do movies today depict the American style of being friendly, open, and optimistic? What examples from recent movies can you think of that show Americans as being friendly, open, and optimistic? How else are Americans portrayed in movies today? Do you think the image of Americans that is portrayed in movies is an accurate reflection of the way Americans are in real life? Why or why not?

READING 4   The Martians Are Coming

Radio was an inexpensive and popular form of entertainment during the Depression years. It was also a powerful force that was able to influence the way people thought. Read this article to learn how a radio show in 1938 was powerful enough to affect millions of listeners and create nationwide panic.

CULTURE KERNEL

The 1930s was an artistic "golden age" for the movie industry. **Gone with the Wind** *and* **The Wizard of Oz***, both released in 1939, are still two of the most popular movies of all time.*

BEFORE YOU READ

Discuss these questions with your classmates.

1. Do you enjoy watching scary movies or reading scary books?

2. What is the scariest movie you have ever seen? What is the scariest book you have ever read?

3. Describe a movie, TV show, or book that frightened you.

---

[2]Michael Barone, "The American Century," *U.S. News & World Report,* December 27, 1999, 42.

The Martians Are Coming

Orson Welles, famous actor, movie director, and radio broadcaster

1   The most famous radio broadcast in history took place at 8:00 P.M. on October 30, 1938. It was Halloween eve, and millions of Americans turned on their radios to listen to a popular program starring Orson Welles. The program that evening was an adaptation of a science fiction story called *The War of the Worlds*. Welles thought that this story about a Martian invasion of Earth would be a good one for the night before Halloween. But Welles decided to make some changes in the original story. For example, he changed the setting from London in the 1890s to present-day New Jersey. Welles also made the show sound like an actual news broadcast about a real invasion from Mars to make it seem more realistic and scary.

2   The show began with an orchestra playing dance music. After a few minutes, the music was interrupted with a "news bulletin" reporting that a "huge flaming object" had landed in New Jersey. The music continued, but "news bulletins" kept interrupting with "live" reports from the scene. During the show, actors pretending to be news announcers and policemen described in great detail the terrifying invasion from Mars.

3   An announcer stated at the beginning of the show that the program was a fictional dramatization. Unfortunately, many listeners tuned in after the show had begun and missed the announcement. They were shocked and afraid when they heard that Martians had landed in the United States. They thought they were listening to a real news bulletin. Thousands of frightened Americans believed that an actual invasion of Earth was taking place. The program was so realistic that they thought they could really hear the Martians and smell their poison gas. Some people packed their suitcases, got into their cars, and attempted to escape. Others tried to defend themselves from the aliens by hiding in basements, loading guns, even wrapping their heads in wet towels to protect themselves from Martian poison gas.

4   Stories of panic caused by the radio show appeared all over the country. The next day, Welles held a press conference. He apologized that his broadcast had caused so many people to panic.

BUILD YOUR TEST-TAKING SKILLS

Circle the letter of the choice that best completes each sentence or answers the question.

1. The article mainly discusses _____.
   a. a real Martian invasion
   b. the history of radio in the United States
   c. a radio broadcast that caused many people to panic
   d. how to protect yourself from poison gas

2. According to the article, _____.
   a. broadcasting can have a powerful effect on its audience
   b. most Americans are still afraid of invasions from other planets
   c. Orson Welles was not sorry for the panic his show had caused
   d. broadcasting rarely has an effect on its audience

3. Which of the following is not a conclusion you can make based on the article?
   a. The original *War of the Worlds* story took place in London in the late nineteenth century.
   b. Radio broadcasts can be made to sound very realistic.
   c. Policemen often appeared on Orson Welles's shows.
   d. People believed Martians use poison gas as a weapon.

4. Where does the author describe some people's reactions to the program?
   a. Paragraph 1   c. Paragraph 3
   b. Paragraph 2   d. Paragraph 4

5. Where does the author discuss two changes Welles made in the original story so his broadcast would seem more realistic?
   a. Paragraph 1   c. Paragraph 3
   b. Paragraph 2   d. Paragraph 4

6. The word *actual* in the last sentence of paragraph 1 means _____.
   a. scary   c. real
   b. loud   d. fake

7. The word *they* in the third sentence of paragraph 3 refers to _____.
   a. policemen   c. invaders
   b. listeners   d. Martians

8. The word *escape* in the seventh sentence of paragraph 3 means _____.
   a. run away   c. fight
   b. hide   d. protect

BUILD YOUR READING SKILLS: Summarizing

On a separate piece of paper, write a one-paragraph summary of Reading 4. Follow these steps:

1. Read the whole article again carefully.

2. Underline the important points in the article.

3. Make a list of the important facts in the article. Try to include *who*, *what*, *when*, *where*, and *why* in your list.

4. Use your list as a guide to write the summary.

LINKING PAST TO PRESENT In the 1930s, radio was a strong force with the power to influence the way people thought. Today, television and the Internet also hold the power to influence public opinion.

REACT AND RESPOND What other examples can you give that show how the media influence the public? Do you think it is positive or negative that the media have so much power? Do you think the government should regulate the media?

HISTORY MAKER: Franklin Delano Roosevelt

Carefully read the list of facts about Franklin Delano Roosevelt, the thirty-second president of the United States. Then choose the information you want from the list to write a paragraph about him on a separate piece of paper. Be sure to begin your paragraph with a topic sentence that states the main idea. Include transition words to guide the reader from one point to the next.

- guided the United States through the Great Depression and World War II
- born in 1882 to wealthy parents
- was fifth cousin of Theodore Roosevelt
- graduated from Harvard College with a major in history
- graduated from Columbia University Law School
- paralyzed by polio in 1921

Franklin Delano Roosevelt, thirty-second president of the United States

- served as governor of New York
- served as thirty-second president of the United States
- promised Americans he would help the country through the Depression
- was a master of communication
- held "fireside chats" with the country by radio
- gave people hope and confidence
- had a strong personality and a lot of self-confidence
- loved being president
- had a great sense of humor
- died while president in 1945

Exchange paragraphs with a partner. Read your partner's paragraph and check it for correct grammar, punctuation, and capitalization.

SKILL REVIEW: Summarizing

Read the passage about the Dust Bowl and complete the exercise that follows.

The Dust Bowl

1   The Great Depression was not the only problem the United States experienced in the 1930s. Another serious problem was the Dust Bowl, resulting from a series of destructive wind and dust storms that hurt farmers on the Great Plains. The strong winds just picked the dusty soil up and blew it in great walls of dirt, killing or ruining everything in its path. People, animals, trees, crops, cars, and machinery were buried under tons of dirt. The worst storms struck Colorado, Kansas, New Mexico, Oklahoma, and Texas, where wheat was the main crop. The soil had become especially dry and loose because wheat did not protect the ground from high winds as the original grasses had done. In addition, there were too many animals feeding in the area, and there had been a severe drought for several years. Many farm families lost everything. More than 30,000 families abandoned the land that their ancestors had farmed for many years and moved farther west to California. Beginning in 1935, the federal government stepped in to help. Programs were set up to send financial aid, plant trees to reduce the force of the winds, and teach farmers how to protect the soil from erosion.

Farm families lose everything in the Dust Bowl of the 1930s.

Write a short summary of the passage on the lines.

_____

_____

_____

PUT IT TOGETHER

Discuss the questions.

1. Climate has a strong effect on many aspects of culture. For example, climate influences the kinds of clothes and even the colors we choose to wear. It also influences eating habits, architecture, and economic development. Discuss effects of climate on a geographic area that you know.

2. In 1938, thousands of people panicked when they heard on the radio that Martians were invading New Jersey. Do you think there could be life on other planets? Why or why not?

3. Will Rogers said, "Good luck, Mr. Ford. It will take a hundred years to tell whether you have helped or hurt us." Cars have not yet been around for 100 years, but they have been around long enough for us to comment on their impact on society. Discuss the ways that cars have helped and hurt society.

CHAPTER 7

WAR AND RECOVERY

The 1940s and 1950s

*I*n this chapter, you will read about the changes in the population, economy, and culture that took place in the United States after World War II.

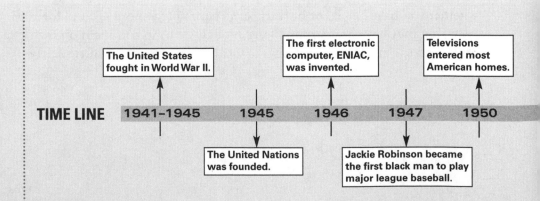

MAKE A CONNECTION

What was happening in your country between 1940 and 1959?

TIME LINE

| 1941–1945 | 1945 | 1946 | 1947 | 1950 |

The United States fought in World War II.

The first electronic computer, ENIAC, was invented.

Televisions entered most American homes.

The United Nations was founded.

Jackie Robinson became the first black man to play major league baseball.

The United States in the 1940s and 1950s

During the 1940s and 1950s, the United States faced both domestic and international challenges as it grew in population and expanded economically.

World War II

The Depression ended when the United States entered World War II. At first, the United States did not want to enter the war, which had begun in Europe in 1939. But in 1941, the United States did enter the war, and the American people, just as they did in World War I, united in support of the war effort. More women than ever before joined the workforce as men left their jobs to fight. The United States emerged from World War II as a major military power. The postwar world became divided into two groups: the capitalist, led by the United States, and the communist, led by the Soviet Union. Tensions between these two groups led to fear and the threat of nuclear war.

The Baby Boom and Postwar Prosperity

After the war, the men came home, and many women left their jobs and returned to homemaking. Young couples moved to the suburbs, where there were newer houses, open spaces, and better schools. So many babies were born at this time that they were called "baby boomers." Because of their numbers, baby boomers have affected American society at every stage of their lives.

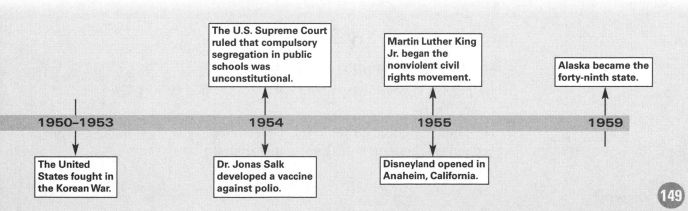

The U.S. Supreme Court ruled that compulsory segregation in public schools was unconstitutional.

Martin Luther King Jr. began the nonviolent civil rights movement.

Alaska became the forty-ninth state.

1950–1953   1954   1955   1959

The United States fought in the Korean War.

Dr. Jonas Salk developed a vaccine against polio.

Disneyland opened in Anaheim, California.

The postwar period was a time of prosperity for many white Americans. People were eager to buy products that they could not afford during the Depression and the war. New labor-saving appliances such as washing machines and dishwashers were in high demand. Popular culture changed dramatically during the 1950s. Watching television became the most popular at-home entertainment. Teenagers turned to a new type of music, rock and roll, that symbolized the youth culture.

The Civil Rights Movement

While millions of Americans prospered, many still lived in poverty. Black Americans still suffered from discrimination in jobs, housing, voting, and education. For example, in some states it was illegal for blacks and whites to eat in the same room in restaurants, use the same bathrooms, or go to the same schools. Gradually a civil rights movement began. Millions of black Americans demanded that segregation end. They fought to be granted their full rights as citizens of the United States.

Despite the domestic and international problems that challenged the United States during the 1940s and 1950s, the country entered the second half of the century with great expectations.

CULTURE KERNEL

In World War II, the Allies included Great Britain, China, France, the Soviet Union, and the United States. The Axis powers included Germany, Italy, and Japan.

Answer the questions.

1. When did the Depression end? _____

2. Why did young couples move to the suburbs? _____

3. Who are the baby boomers? _____

4. Why did a civil rights movement begin? _____

READING 1   Raising the Baby Boomers

In the late 1940s and early 1950s, there was a huge increase in the birthrate in the United States. This produced a generation that is called the baby boomers. In this article, you will read about how parenting changed in the 1950s.

BEFORE YOU READ

Discuss these questions with your classmates.

1. Do parents in your country tend to be strict or permissive? Give some examples.

2. How much freedom do you think parents should give their young children? School-age children? Teenagers? Young adults?

Raising the Baby Boomers

1   Veterans returning home from World War II were usually eager to resume their lives. For most, that meant starting a family. Between 1946 and 1960, 63 million babies were born in the United States, up 22 million from the fifteen-year period before that. This steep jump in the birthrate came to be known as the baby boom.

2   Before the war, American children were raised very strictly. They were often told to be "seen and not heard." After the war, however, young parents raised their children according to different ideas. Dr. Benjamin Spock's *Common Sense Book of Baby and Child Care*, published in 1946, emphasized flexibility in raising children. Spock encouraged parents to listen to their children and respond to their wishes. New parents quickly made Dr. Spock's book the best-selling book in U.S. history. By 1952, sales had reached 4 million copies and continued at a rate of 1 million copies per year for the next eighteen years.

3   Critics who believed that the old ways of raising children were best accused Spock of being too permissive. They thought his ideas would spoil children. But Spock opposed harsh discipline because he thought there was "no such thing as a bad boy." By this he meant that, although a child's *behavior* may be bad, the *child* is not. Millions of baby boom parents were influenced by Spock's advice, which revolutionized the way children were raised.

BUILD YOUR TEST-TAKING SKILLS

Circle the letter of the choice that best completes each sentence.

1. The article mainly discusses _____.
   a. how children were raised before World War II
   b. the influence of Dr. Spock on the way baby boom children were raised
   c. the benefits of harsh discipline on children
   d. the impact of baby boomers on the economy

2. According to the article, Spock's ideas _____.
   a. revolutionized child-rearing practices in the United States
   b. were too permissive
   c. were old-fashioned
   d. caused the baby boom

3. Spock believed that _____.
   a. many children were born bad
   b. parents should be strict with their children
   c. parents should spoil their children
   d. a child's behavior might be bad, but the child is not

4. Spock's book encouraged parents to _____.
   a. spoil their children
   b. have fewer children
   c. listen to their children and respond to their needs
   d. watch their children carefully, but not listen to them

5. The word *they* in the second sentence of paragraph 3 refers to
   _____.
   a. critics of Spock   c. parents of baby boomers
   b. supporters of Spock   d. baby boomer children

6. The word *jump* in the last sentence of paragraph 1 means _____.
   a. hop   c. skip
   b. decrease   d. increase

BUILD YOUR READING SKILLS: Distinguishing Fact from Opinion

It is important to be able to distinguish between a fact and an opinion. A *fact* is something that happened or a statement that can be proven. An *opinion*, on the other hand, is someone's belief, feeling, or judgment.

*If the statement is a fact, write **F** on the line. If it is an opinion, write **O**.*

_____ 1. More than 60 million babies were born in the United States between 1946 and 1960.

_____ 2. It is better for children to be seen and not heard.

_____ 3. The number of babies born in the United States increased dramatically after World War II.

_____ 4. Dr. Spock's method of raising children is too permissive.

_____ 5. Spock's ideas spoil children.

_____ 6. Dr. Spock's *Common Sense Book of Baby and Child Care* had sold 4 million copies by 1952.

_____ 7. *Common Sense Book of Baby and Child Care* is the best book on child rearing ever written.

_____ 8. Spock opposed harsh discipline of children.

_____ 9. Strict discipline is not good for children.

Today, many of Dr. Spock's theories are still widely accepted. But the world is a very different place from what it was in the 1950s when Dr. Spock supported full-time motherhood. At that time, he believed that mothers should stay at home and take care of their children. Now, many mothers work outside the home. Children have baby-sitters or go to child care. Dr. Spock might not have agreed with this, but his ideas were a reflection of the values of his time.

REACT AND RESPOND Do you think it is all right for mothers to work outside the home? What kind of child care do you think is the best? What are the advantages and disadvantages of children going to child care and preschool programs?

READING 2 TV Takes Off

At the beginning of the 1950s, only a small number of Americans owned television sets, but by the end of the decade, TVs were found in most homes. Television changed both the way people spent their free time and the way that information was communicated. In this article, you will get a look into television in the 1950s.

BEFORE YOU READ

Discuss these questions with your classmates.

1. On average, how many hours of television do you watch per day?

2. What kinds of television shows do you prefer, for example, news, comedies, movies, or sports?

3. Do you think television will have a greater or lesser impact on society in the future?

TV Takes Off
by Richard Steins

A 1950s family gathers in front of their TV.

1   One of the most dramatic changes to affect everyday life in America in the 1950s was the growth of television. In 1950, only 21 percent of the entire country had TV sets. By 1955, about 66 percent of the population owned TVs, and by the 1960s, that number had risen to approximately 87 percent. By the end of the decade, Americans owned more TVs than refrigerators.

2   When few Americans had TVs at the beginning of the 1950s, people would gather at the home of a family that had a TV in order to watch a favorite program. But soon, more and more people owned TVs, and eventually, typical family entertainment involved gathering around the television at home in the evening. In 1954, an American food company invented the first "TV dinner," which was supposed to allow people to continue watching their favorite programs rather than stopping to cook and eat.

3   Throughout the 1950s, as TV became more and more popular, attendance at movie theaters declined. Although TV watching tended to encourage isolation from contact beyond the family, TV also brought Americans together by generating a new widespread culture in the United States. At the beginning of the TV age, there were three or four network channels. Public television did not start until the 1960s, and cable TV was not

widely popular until the 1980s. As a result, people all over the country—whether they lived in the North, South, East, or West—watched the same shows and saw the same advertisements each evening.

4   Television's early shows helped create a uniform pop culture as they reflected the America of the 1950s. The most popular show of the 1950s was *I Love Lucy*, which revolved around the adventures of a wacky New York housewife named Lucy Ricardo and her Cuban-born husband, Ricky. Lucy was a housewife of the 1950s. Ricky did not want her to work, but Lucy was always scheming to get her own way. Lucy was played by Lucille Ball (1911–1989), and Ricky was her actual husband, Desi Arnez (1917–1986). When the couple had a child in 1957, the event was written into the script of the TV show. Some 45 million people watched the show on which Lucy the character had a baby. Today, many of television's classic and historic shows can be seen in reruns. *I Love Lucy* still plays in almost every city around the country, forty years after it first appeared.

5   Other TV shows of the times—such as *Father Knows Best* and *Leave It to Beaver*—offered an unrealistic view of life as they showed fathers who worked at unnamed jobs and who sat around the house in ties and jackets. Mothers had no outside jobs but stayed at home while they baked, wearing high-heeled shoes and jewelry. Television of the 1950s often portrayed a fantasy world where there was no poverty, death, rebellion, ethnic mixing, or racial tension.

6   Since the early days of television, people have debated its effects on society. Some people see it as a negative and passive influence causing people to simply stare at a screen for hours instead of engaging in other stimulating or productive activities. Others, however, see television's positive influences—particularly its quick access to information through news programs and its educational uses, especially since the beginning of public TV and cable networks.

CHECK YOUR COMPREHENSION

Check (✓) the items that are true for the 1950s.

_____ 1. Americans owned more TVs than refrigerators.

_____ 2. The number of people who went to movie theaters decreased.

_____ 3. Public television began.

_____ 4. *I Love Lucy* was the most popular TV show.

_____ 5. Television showed a lot of ethnic mixing.

_____ 6. Television portrayed a very realistic world.

_____ 7. There were ten network channels.

EXPAND YOUR VOCABULARY

Complete each sentence with the correct form of a word from the list.

1. entertain, entertainer, entertaining, entertainment
   a. Barbra Streisand is my favorite musical _____.
   b. My neighbors like to _____ on weekends.
   c. What is your favorite form of _____?
   d. The movie that we saw last night was very _____.

2. invent, inventor, invention, inventive
   a. The fax machine is an amazing _____.
   b. Who _____ the lightbulb?
   c. He is one of the most _____ musicians alive today.
   d. I would love to be a famous _____.

3. continue, continuation, continuous, continually, continuing
   a. Their _____ arguing upsets me.
   b. They argue _____.
   c. Tonight's show is a _____ of last night's program.
   d. The government predicts that the population will _____ to grow.
   e. Classes for adult learners are often called _____ education.

4. encourage, encouragement, encouraging
   a. My teacher _____ me to try out for our school play.
   b. The news from the doctors is very _____.
   c. She needed a lot of _____, but she finally succeeded.

BUILD YOUR READING SKILLS: Scanning

Scan the article to find answers to the questions.

1. What percentage of the population owned TV sets by 1960?

   _____

2. When was the first TV dinner invented? _____

3. Who was Lucille Ball's husband? _____

4. What were the names of two TV shows in the 1950s besides *I Love Lucy*?

   _____

   _____

5. When was Lucille Ball born? _____ When did she die?

_____

6. When did cable TV become widely popular? _____

7. By 1955, about what percentage of the population owned TVs?

_____

BUILD YOUR SKILLS: Paraphrasing

Paraphrasing *is rewriting someone else's sentences in your own words.*
Paraphrase these sentences from Reading 2. Your sentences should express the
main idea of the original sentence as clearly and simply as possible.

> **Example:** When few Americans had TVs at the beginning of the 1950s,
> people would gather at the home of a family that had a TV in
> order to watch a favorite program.
>
> *At the beginning of the 1950s, most people did not own TVs, so they*
> *would go to a friend's house to watch TV.*

1. One of the most dramatic changes to affect everyday life in America in the
1950s was the growth of television.

_____

_____

2. In 1954, an American food company invented the first "TV dinner," which
was supposed to allow people to continue watching their favorite programs
rather than stopping to cook and eat.

_____

_____

3. Mothers had no outside jobs but stayed at home while they baked, wearing
high-heeled shoes and jewelry.

_____

_____

4. Some people see it as a negative and passive influence causing people to
simply stare at a screen for hours instead of engaging in other stimulating
or productive activities.

_____

_____

BUILD YOUR READING SKILLS: Understanding Transitions

Read the sentences from Reading 2 and underline the transitions. Write the transition word(s) on the line and identify the type of relationship it signifies. Refer to the chart on page 36.

1. Throughout the 1950s, as TV became more and more popular, attendance at movie theaters declined.

   Transition: _____   Type of relationship: _____

   Transition: _____   Type of relationship: _____

2. Although TV watching tended to encourage isolation from contact beyond the family, TV also bonded Americans together by generating a new widespread culture in the United States.

   Transition: _____   Type of relationship: _____

   Transition: _____   Type of relationship: _____

3. Other TV shows of the times—such as *Father Knows Best* and *Leave It to Beaver*—offered an unrealistic view of life as they showed fathers who worked at unnamed jobs and who sat around the house in ties and jackets.

   Transition: _____   Type of relationship: _____

   Transition: _____   Type of relationship: _____

   Transition: _____   Type of relationship: _____

4. As a result, people all over the country—whether they lived in the North, South, East, or West—watched the same shows and saw the same advertisements each evening.

   Transition: _____   Type of relationship: _____

   Transition: _____   Type of relationship: _____

   Transition: _____   Type of relationship: _____

5. Since the early days of television, people have debated its effects on society.

   Transition: _____   Type of relationship: _____

 LINKING PAST TO PRESENT Today, television is so much a part of most of our lives that we forget it has not been around for very long. Whether you believe that watching television is a waste of time or a powerful educational tool, you will probably agree that it is among the most significant inventions of our time.

REACT AND RESPOND How was the invention of television similar to the invention of the printing press, the automobile, or the computer? How have each of these inventions changed our lives?

Rock and roll has been the greatest commercial success of any music style in history. This article describes how rock and roll developed in the 1950s.

BEFORE YOU READ

Discuss these questions with your classmates.

1. Do you like rock music? Why or why not?

2. Who is your favorite rock musician?

3. Do you think rock music has a positive or negative effect on young people?

Rock and Roll and the Power of Youth
by Richard Steins

Elvis Presley, the king of rock and roll

1   If television was one of the great influences of cultural change in the 1950s, another was the emergence of rock-and-roll music. Rock in the 1950s was a blend of white country-and-western music and black-inspired rhythm and blues. It caught on quickly and became an established feature of American culture.

2   American teenagers of the 1950s, unlike those of earlier generations, had their own money to spend. Certain industries—especially the record industry—understood that a new teen market was growing and becoming an economic force. Between 1953 and 1959, record sales increased from $213 million to more than $600 million, with teenage consumers as the driving force. Rock quickly became the leading music sold on records.

3   In addition to music, other industries were focusing on the new "youth culture" of the time. With television viewing

(continues on next page)

growing dramatically, audiences at movie theaters consisted largely of teenagers, who had money to spend and enjoyed time away from their homes. Movies such as *Rebel without a Cause* and *The Wild One*, starring reckless young actors such as James Dean (1931–1955) and Marlon Brando (1924–) romanticized the rebelliousness of youth.

4   Rock and roll, with its driving beat, wildly loud delivery, and lyrics about things that mattered to teens, was a perfect new music for the age. The first rock-and-roll record to achieve nationwide fame was "Rock around the Clock" by Bill Haley and the Comets, released in 1955. But it was a young man from Tupelo, Mississippi, named Elvis Presley (1935–1977), who brought rock and roll into everyone's living room in 1956. Presley was comfortable singing country and western as well as rhythm and blues and gospel music. According to one record company executive, Presley was a white man who had a "black sound." Presley's earliest hits included "Hound Dog," "Heartbreak Hotel," "Don't Be Cruel," and "Love Me Tender." The latter was also the title of his first movie, made in 1956. The most dramatic moment in Presley's early career was his nationwide appearance on the *Ed Sullivan Show* in 1956. Before a studio audience of screaming girls, Presley performed "Hound Dog." The television audience saw him only from the waist up. (There was public objection over the way Presley moved and shook his hips on stage.)

5   To many adults, rock-and-roll music was shocking. It represented everything that was wrong with the young, especially their rebellion against authority. But rock firmly established itself as a part of American culture. Eventually, rock music went through a number of very different transformations as it was molded by such artists as the Beatles, Bob Dylan, Jimi Hendrix, and many others. In the end, however, the growth of rock music, more than anything else, represented the increasing influence of the young in cultural expression and a major shift in musical taste.

CHECK YOUR COMPREHENSION

A. *Mark each item true (**T**) or false (**F**).*

_____ **1.** Rock and roll was a mixture of country-and-western music and rhythm and blues.

_____ **2.** Rock music took a long time to become popular.

_____ **3.** Teenagers before the 1950s rarely had a lot of money to spend.

_____ **4.** Music was the only industry to focus on the new "youth culture" of the time.

_____ **5.** Elvis Presley's early hit "Hound Dog" was the first rock-and-roll record to achieve nationwide fame.

_____ **6.** Many adults in the 1950s thought rock-and-roll music was shocking.

B. *Circle the letter of the choice that best completes each sentence.*

1. Elvis Presley was comfortable singing _____ music.
   - **a.** gospel
   - **b.** country-and-western
   - **c.** rhythm-and-blues
   - **d.** all of the above

2. The title of Presley's first movie was _____.
   - **a.** *Hound Dog*
   - **b.** *Heartbreak Hotel*
   - **c.** *Don't Be Cruel*
   - **d.** *Love Me Tender*

3. An artist that is not mentioned as an example of a rock-and-roll musician is _____.
   - **a.** Jimi Hendrix
   - **b.** Hank Williams
   - **c.** the Beatles
   - **d.** Bob Dylan

4. _____ was the leading music sold on records in the 1950s.
   - **a.** Blues
   - **b.** Country
   - **c.** Rock and roll
   - **d.** Gospel

EXPAND YOUR VOCABULARY

Circle the two words in each row that are antonyms.

1. always	quickly	sadly	slowly
2. spend	change	fear	save
3. prices	sales	purchases	goals
4. disturbing	losing	growing	shrinking
5. loud	full	soft	effective
6. longest	most	busiest	least
7. previous	early	before	late
8. wrong	difficult	sensible	right
9. coldly	firmly	originally	loosely
10. good	less	more	worse

CULTURE KERNEL

Twenty percent of the population at the time of George Washington's inauguration in 1789 was black. In the 1990s, African Americans made up 12 percent of the U.S. population but remained the country's largest ethnic minority.[1]

LINKING PAST TO PRESENT Most adults were horrified by Elvis Presley. They disapproved of the way he danced, and they couldn't understand the songs he sang. Many parents did not want their teenage children to go to his concerts or listen to his records. Some radio stations even refused to play his music. Today, most adults accept rock and roll, but they disapprove of new music such as rap because some of the songs are about sex, drugs, and gangs.

REACT AND RESPOND Do you think radio stations should play music that is about sex, drugs, and gangs? Do you think these songs influence the behavior of teenagers?

[1]John Elson, "The Great Migration," *Time*, Fall Special Issue, 1993, 28.

The 1950s were a period of progress for black Americans as they struggled to achieve racial equality by ending segregation and discrimination. A civil rights movement was born during this time. Its most famous leader, Martin Luther King Jr., believed that blacks should try to change society and its laws through nonviolent means. In this article, you will read about some of the victories blacks won and important advances the movement has made.

Highlights of the Civil Rights Movement

Rosa Parks, civil rights activist

1954: *OLIVER BROWN V. BOARD OF EDUCATION OF TOPEKA, KANSAS*

1   In the 1950s, school segregation was still common across the country. In fact, in most southern states, it was illegal for black and white children to attend the same school. In 1952, a number of school segregation cases, such as *Brown* v. *Board of Education of Topeka, Kansas*, came before the Supreme Court. In 1954, the Supreme Court ruled that laws requiring separate schools for black children were unconstitutional. As a result, it became illegal for states to segregate children in public schools. This ruling was an important victory for blacks.

1955: MONTGOMERY BUS BOYCOTT

2   On December 1, 1955, a forty-two-year-old black woman named Rosa Parks was waiting for her bus in Montgomery, Alabama. She was tired after a hard day at work, and when the bus came, she got on and sat down in the section for whites. At that time, there was a law in Alabama that required black people to sit in the back of the bus and to give up their seats if a white person needed a place to sit. When the bus began to fill up with passengers, the bus driver told Rosa to move to the rear of the bus so a white man could have her seat. Rosa Parks refused to move. She was arrested and put in jail. The following night, leaders of the black community, including Dr. Martin Luther King Jr., met to discuss the issue. The leaders announced that Montgomery's black community would refuse to ride the buses until the segregation policies ended. King's house was bombed by angry white citizens, and Rosa Parks was fired from her job, but the bus boycott continued for over a year. Finally, a federal court ordered Montgomery's buses desegregated in November 1956, and the boycott ended in triumph. Many people believe that the civil rights movement began with the Montgomery bus boycott in 1955.

1960: Sit-ins

3   Even in the 1960s, many restaurants and other public places were still segregated. On February 1, 1960, four black college students sat at a "whites only" lunch counter in Greensboro, North Carolina, and demanded service. When they were not served, they stayed in their seats. The students decided to "sit-in" until they were served. They would not leave even when customers poured food on them and tried to push them off their stools. Finally, the police came and arrested them. An article in the *New York Times* drew attention to the sit-in, and soon students across the country began to participate in other nonviolent protests. In the next two months, similar sit-ins occurred in fifty-four cities in nine states. As a result, many restaurants were desegregated. The sit-in movement also showed Americans that young blacks were serious about ending segregation.

1963: March on Washington

4   On August 28, 1963, over 250,000 people met in Washington, D.C., for the biggest civil rights demonstration in U.S. history. Martin Luther King Jr. and other black leaders had organized the March on Washington as a massive protest for jobs and civil rights. King delivered his moving "I Have a Dream" speech to more than 200,000 civil rights supporters. In his speech, King expressed the hopes of the civil rights movement: "I have a dream that one day this nation will rise up and live out the true meaning of its creed: 'We hold these truths to be self-evident, that all men are created equal.' . . . I have a dream that my four little children will one day live in a nation where they will not be judged by the color of their skin but by the content of their character." This historic event came to symbolize the civil rights movement. It resulted in the Civil Rights Act of 1964, which prohibited segregation in public places, as well as discrimination in education and employment.

1965: Voting Rights Act

5   In the mid-1960s, many states still limited the right of black people to vote. One law said that a person must be able to read and write in order to vote. This disqualified the many blacks who had not attended school. Another law required voters to own property, something few blacks were able to do. Finally, there was a law that required voters to pay a tax before they voted. But since most southern blacks were very poor, they could not pay the tax. On August 6, President Lyndon B. Johnson signed the Voting Rights Act of 1965, which put an end to literacy tests. The passage of the Voting Rights Act allowed blacks to exercise their constitutional right to vote. The effects of the Voting Rights Act in the South were remarkable. In the three years following its passage, almost a million more blacks in the South registered to vote. By 1968, black voters had a significant impact on southern politics.

CHECK YOUR COMPREHENSION

Complete the chart with the numbers of the items from the list.

1. allowed blacks to use their constitutional right to vote
2. ended discrimination in education and employment
3. gave blacks a voice in politics
4. resulted in the desegregation of many restaurants
5. showed Americans that young blacks were serious about ending segregation
6. made laws requiring separate schools for black children unconstitutional
7. prohibited segregation in public places
8. put an end to literacy tests
9. resulted in integration of public schools
10. ended segregation on public buses
11. resulted in the Civil Rights Act of 1964
12. was the biggest civil rights demonstration in U.S. history
13. inspired by Rosa Parks's arrest
14. included King's "I Have a Dream" speech

BROWN V. BOARD OF ED.	MONTGOMERY BUS BOYCOTT	SIT-INS	MARCH ON WASHINGTON	CIVIL RIGHTS ACT OF 1964	VOTING RIGHTS ACT

LINKING PAST TO PRESENT

"The situation of blacks in America is a unique one. No other group to come here from a foreign continent was so completely torn away from its roots, and no other group had to endure slavery. . . . The struggle of blacks to gain civil rights—both before and after slavery—has been one of ups and downs. Gains toward full justice and opportunity have been made, lost, and made again. Many political compromises, court battles, and laws have been part of the struggle. . . . [T]he civil rights of blacks are now guaranteed by law. But because opportunities for blacks have become available only in more recent times, blacks are often the first to suffer during hard times when opportunities and money are short. . . . And so the struggle goes on—a struggle that is not only for improvements for blacks or individual minority groups, but for the improvement of all America."[2]

REACT AND RESPOND Is racism a problem in your country?

---

[2]"The View from the Crow's Nest," *Cobblestone*, February 1983: 5.

HISTORY MAKER: Martin Luther King Jr.

Read the list of facts about Martin Luther King Jr. Then choose the information you want from the list to write a paragraph about him on a separate piece of paper. Be sure to begin your paragraph with a topic sentence that states the main idea. Include transition words to guide the reader from one point to the next.

Martin Luther King Jr., leader of the civil rights movement

- believed in freedom and equality for all people
- born in 1929 in Atlanta, Georgia
- was African-American minister with strong religious beliefs
- led nonviolent protests such as sit-ins and marches all over the country to end segregation and gain equality
- expressed African Americans' desires for civil rights and social justice
- inspired by transcendentalists such as Henry David Thoreau and Mohandas Gandhi
- was main leader of the civil rights movement in the United States during 1950s and 1960s
- gained national attention with bus boycott in 1955 in Montgomery, Alabama
- was an excellent public speaker
- led March on Washington in 1963 for passage of civil rights legislation
- won Nobel Peace Prize in 1964 for his use of nonviolence to achieve equality
- led freedom march in Alabama in support of Voting Rights Act of 1965
- was assassinated during a protest march in 1968 in Memphis, Tennessee

Exchange your paragraph with a partner. Read your partner's paragraph and check it for correct grammar, punctuation, and capitalization.

SKILL REVIEW: Distinguishing Fact from Opinion

Read the passage about Alaska and complete the exercise.

Alaska has spectacular views.

Alaska

1   In 1867, soon after the Civil War, Russia wanted to sell the area now known as Alaska to the United States. Secretary of State William H. Seward signed an agreement to buy Alaska for the low price of $7.2 million—less than two cents per acre (five cents per hectare). Despite the inexpensive price, Seward was severely criticized for wasting so much money on ice and snow. People laughed at him and referred to Alaska as "Seward's Folly" and "Seward's Icebox." Thirty years later, however, in 1896, it became obvious that Seward's purchase had been a good investment for the country. Gold was discovered in Alaska, and thousands of people rushed there hoping to get rich. Besides gold, they found that Alaska was also rich in fish, furs, trees, minerals, gas, and oil. It is a beautiful, rugged land of high mountains, icy glaciers, active volcanoes, dense forests, and treeless islands. Alaska became the country's forty-ninth and largest state in 1959.

If the statement is a fact, write **F** *on the line. If it is an opinion, write* **O**.

_____ 1. The United States bought Alaska from Russia.

_____ 2. The United States paid less than two cents per acre for Alaska.

_____ 3. Secretary of State William H. Seward spent too much money on Alaska.

_____ 4. Alaska has many valuable natural resources.

_____ 5. Alaska is the most beautiful state in the United States.

PUT IT TOGETHER

Discuss the questions.

1. In what ways does television shape opinions about the news? In what ways does television reflect the culture?

2. How much freedom do teenagers have in your country? How much freedom do you think they should have?

3. American middle-class society became a consumer culture during the 1950s. Today, American society is still characterized by consumerism and the accumulation of material wealth and goods. Do you think consumerism is good or bad? How does it affect the way people lead their lives?

4. There are currently approximately 75 million members of the baby boom generation in the United States. Experts have predicted for a long time that there will be tremendous changes in the United States as the baby boomers grow old and retire and as science helps people live longer. What sort of changes do you predict in housing, politics, family structure, and health care?

5. What do you think are the best ways to fight racism? Do you believe nonviolent means such as the ones Martin Luther King Jr. supported are the most effective? How can education be used as a tool to combat racism?

CHAPTER 8

TURBULENT TIMES

The 1960s and 1970s

In this chapter, you will learn that the 1960s and 1970s were an exciting and revolutionary period of technological advances and social change.

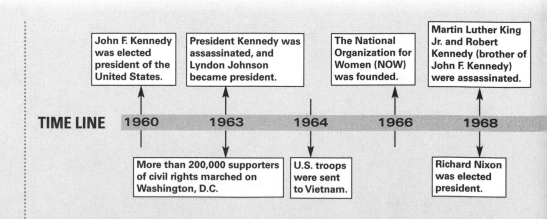

MAKE A CONNECTION

What was happening in your country between 1960 and 1979?

TIME LINE

| 1960 | 1963 | 1964 | 1966 | 1968 |

John F. Kennedy was elected president of the United States.

President Kennedy was assassinated, and Lyndon Johnson became president.

The National Organization for Women (NOW) was founded.

Martin Luther King Jr. and Robert Kennedy (brother of John F. Kennedy) were assassinated.

More than 200,000 supporters of civil rights marched on Washington, D.C.

U.S. troops were sent to Vietnam.

Richard Nixon was elected president.

The United States in the 1960s and 1970s

The 1960s and 1970s in the United States were characterized by social upheaval and technological advances.

Social and Cultural Upheaval at Home and War Overseas

The 1960s was a period of social and cultural revolution. Almost 40 percent of all Americans were under the age of forty. Millions of young people became concerned about injustices in American society and decided to challenge the values of older generations. More and more people came to believe that the United States should not be involved in a civil war in another country, Vietnam. They organized demonstrations to show their opposition to the war.

African Americans continued their struggle for civil rights. Women, Native Americans, Hispanics, gays and lesbians, and people with disabilities were all affected by the civil rights movement. Each group became organized in its fight to end discrimination.

The turmoil of the 1960s continued into the 1970s as many Americans lost faith in their leaders and government. After years of fighting in Vietnam, the United States lost its first war. At home, people watched President Richard Nixon resign from office because of a political scandal.

Exploring the Frontiers of Technology

The 1960s and 1970s were a period of technological growth. On July 20, 1969, more than a billion people turned on their TVs to watch the first person set

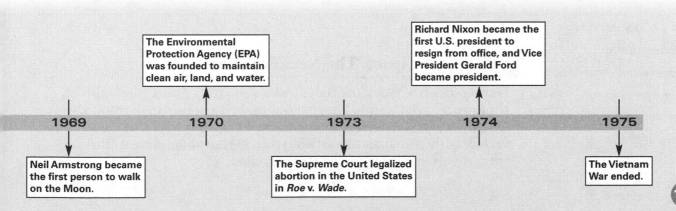

The Environmental Protection Agency (EPA) was founded to maintain clean air, land, and water.

Richard Nixon became the first U.S. president to resign from office, and Vice President Gerald Ford became president.

1969   **1970**   **1973**   **1974**   **1975**

Neil Armstrong became the first person to walk on the Moon.

The Supreme Court legalized abortion in the United States in *Roe* v. *Wade*.

The Vietnam War ended.

foot on the Moon. Back on Earth, the introduction of small, easy-to-use, affordable personal computers started a revolution that changed the daily lives of people all over the world.

The Energy Crisis and the Environmental Movement

During the middle of the 1970s, oil shortages created a huge energy crisis in the United States. This led many Americans to think about conservation and the dangers to the environment from pollution. At the same time, some people who were frustrated with politics turned inward. The growing environmental movement taught them to be concerned with the health of the Earth, and this concern led them to improve their own health as well. Thus, the 1970s are often called the "Me Decade" because Americans became obsessed with their personal lifestyles. They explored the benefits of exercise, health food, and meditation.

Answer the questions.

1. Why were some Americans opposed to the war in Vietnam?

   _____

2. What other groups were affected by the civil rights movements of African Americans?

   a. _____

   b. _____

   c. _____

   d. _____

   e. _____

3. What technological advancements occurred during this time?

   a. _____

   b. _____

4. Why are the 1970s referred to as the "Me Decade?"

   _____

CULTURE KERNEL

In 1977, Star Wars became the most commercially successful film ever made. It revolutionized cinematic special effects.

READING 1 **Space: The Next Frontier**

During the early 1960s, the United States entered a "space race" with the former Soviet Union. The goal was to send a person to the Moon. On July 20, 1969, American astronaut Neil Armstrong set foot on the surface of the Moon. In this article, you will read about some of the space flights that led up to the Moon landing.

AS YOU READ

As you read about America's attempt to finish first in the space race, think about these questions.

1. What did space represent for the United States and the Soviet Union?

2. What qualities did the astronauts have?

3. Why did America's first astronauts become national heroes?

Space: The Next Frontier
By Jack Bealdon

Astronaut John Glenn's Flight into Orbit Captured the Spirit of the 1960s

An astronaut takes a walk on the Moon.

1 The 1960s began bright and clear for America. Although the decade would soon experience an unpopular war in Vietnam, race riots at home, and a series of political assassinations, the early years were marked by optimism and a belief that American know-how could conquer any problem.

(continues on next page)

2   And nothing caught the imagination quite as strongly as America's first group of astronauts, known as the Mercury 7. These patriotic test pilots would carry America's best dreams skyward, pioneering the final frontier—space. The public adored them—especially one astronaut, John Glenn.

3   Their mission: to win the "space race." In 1957, the former Soviet Union (now Russia) had launched the first satellite, called *Sputnik*, into orbit, leaving the United States in second place. And second in space, one politician noted at the time, meant "second in everything." Both sides were looking for a military advantage and considered space a new "platform" from which to launch their deadly missiles. Here, in a series of quotes from major participants, is the story of America's attempt to win the space race.

THE CHALLENGE

4   On April 12, 1961, Russian cosmonaut Yuri Gagarin rode the *Vostok I* around Earth for 108 minutes, becoming the first man in space. President Kennedy used the news to boost America's rocket program, promising $1.7 billion to catch up.

5   This nation should commit itself to achieving the goal, before the decade is out, of landing a man on the Moon and returning him safely to Earth. No single space project will be more important to mankind or more important for the long-range exploration of space; and none will be so difficult or expensive to accomplish.

—John F. Kennedy,
State of the Union Address,
May 25, 1961

AMERICA'S FLYBOYS

6   But it would take more than money. To overtake the Soviets, America turned to a war hero, U.S. Marine Lieutenant Colonel John Glenn Jr., and six other pilots for the honor of becoming America's first astronauts. The country's first spacemen had to be physically fit, excellent pilots, and smart. They also had to represent America's hopes and dreams.

7   They were a group of mature Americans, average in build, family men, college educated, possessing excellent health, and professionally committed to flying advanced aircraft.

—NASA, 1960

THE FLIGHT OF *FRIENDSHIP 7*

8   In 1961, Alan Shepard became the first American in space. But his fifteen-minute up-and-down journey into space didn't achieve orbit. Soviet Premier Nikita Krushchev said that while the Soviets were flying high, America was still learning to jump.

9   The nation looked to John Glenn and his scheduled flight to orbit the Earth. On his shoulders lay the pride and, many believed, the security of the nation.

10   On February 20, 1962, Glenn boarded the *Freedom 7* Mercury spacecraft and the countdown began. On February 20, 1962, Glenn became the first American to orbit the Earth in space, in the Project Mercury Gemini capsule *Friendship 7*. The three-orbit flight covered approximately 130,000 kilometers in approximately five hours.

11   Many people assume astronauts must be deathly afraid prior to a flight, but I didn't look at it that way. . . . We were certainly aware that the tremendously increased speeds, power, and complexities of space travel could put us in danger . . . , but the risks were worth it.

—John Glenn,
My Experience in Space, 1997

A HERO'S RETURN

12   For the people who worked on the Mercury project, Glenn's flight was proof that no job was too complex for NASA. As for Glenn, he returned to a different America than the one he had rocketed away from five hours before. It was as if all the pessimism and fear had been washed away by his brilliant success. Glenn's flight elevated him to superstar status—4 million people lined the streets of New York for a parade.

13   John did not merely get a parade, and a trip to the White House, and a medal from the president. Oh, he got those things all right. But he also addressed a special joint session of Congress—the Senate and the House met together to hear John, the way they had for presidents, prime ministers, and kings. . . . And that was just the start. In a way, that was nothing compared to the big parade in New York.

14   There must have been millions of people out there, packed from curbings clear back to the storefronts, and there were people hanging out of all the windows, particularly along lower Broadway, where the buildings were older and they could open the windows, and they were filling the air with shreds of paper, every piece of paper they could get their hands on.

—Tom Wolfe, *The Right Stuff*

CHECK YOUR COMPREHENSION

A. *Mark each item true (**T**) or false (**F**).*

_____ **1.** The early 1960s were marked by optimism.

_____ **2.** During the 1960s, Americans considered space the final frontier.

_____ **3.** The Soviet Union and the United States worked together to explore the Moon.

_____ **4.** The first man in space was Russian cosmonaut Yuri Gagarin.

_____ **5.** President Kennedy wanted to cut back on the space program.

_____ **6.** In 1961, American astronaut Alan Shepard orbited the Earth.

_____ **7.** John Glenn became a national hero after his flight into space.

B. *Circle the letter of the choice that best completes each sentence.*

1. John Glenn's flight into orbit captured the spirit of the early 1960s because it _____.
   a. helped win the war in Vietnam
   b. cost so much money
   c. reflected the belief that American know-how could conquer any problem
   d. provoked race riots and peace demonstrations

2. President Kennedy's goal in the space race was to be the first to _____.
   a. land a man on the Moon
   b. orbit the Earth
   c. orbit the Moon
   d. put a man in space

3. John Glenn's *Friendship 7* mission took _____ and made _____ around the Earth.
   a. 3 hours; 5 orbits
   b. 7 hours; 5 orbits
   c. 5 hours; 3 orbits
   d. 3 hours; 7 orbits

EXPAND YOUR VOCABULARY

Match each word or phrase from the reading with its antonym.

1. _____ special
2. _____ aware
3. _____ adore
4. _____ joint
5. _____ prior to
6. _____ approximately
7. _____ pessimism
8. _____ difficult
9. _____ professional
10. _____ complex

a. separate
b. optimism
c. exactly
d. ignorant
e. amateur
f. easy
g. hate
h. ordinary
i. simple
j. after

BUILD YOUR READING SKILLS: Scanning

Scan the chart to find answers to the questions.

1. Who was the first woman to travel in space? _____

2. What nationality was she? _____

3. What was the date of the first manned space flight that orbited the Moon?

   _____

4. What major achievement occurred in 1962? _____

5. Who traveled in the first U.S. two-person space flight? _____

6. What did Alexei A. Leonov accomplish? _____

IMPORTANT MANNED SPACE MISSIONS		
DATE	**NAME**	**ACHIEVEMENT**
April 12, 1961	Cosmonaut Yuri A. Gagarin	First person in Earth orbit
May 5, 1961	Astronaut Alan B. Shepard Jr.	First American in space
Feb. 20, 1962	Astronaut John H. Glenn Jr.	First American in Earth orbit
June 16, 1963	Cosmonaut Valentina Tereshkova	First woman in space
March 18, 1965	Cosmonaut Alexei A. Leonov	First person to "walk" in space
March 23, 1965	Astronauts Virgil I. Grissom and John W. Young	First U.S. two-person space flight
June 5, 1965	Astronaut Edward H. White II	First U.S. space walk
Dec. 21, 1968	Astronauts William A. Anders, Frank Borman, and James A. Lovell Jr.	First manned flight around the Moon
July 20, 1969	Astronauts Neil A. Armstrong and Edwin E. Aldrin Jr.	First manned landing on the Moon
June 7, 1971	Cosmonauts Georgi T. Dobrovolsky, Victor I. Patsayev, and Vladislav N. Volkov	First manned orbiting space station
May 25, 1973	Astronauts Charles Conrad Jr., Joseph P. Kerwin, and Paul J. Weitz	First manned U.S. space station
July 15, 1975	Astronauts Vance D. Brand, Donald K. Slayton, and Thomas P. Stafford with cosmonauts Alexei A. Leonov and Valery N. Kubasov	First international space mission (Apollo-Soyuz Test Project)

WRITE ABOUT IT

When Neil Armstrong stepped on the Moon, he said these words: "That's one small step for man, one giant leap for mankind." On a separate piece of paper, write a paragraph describing what he meant.

LINKING PAST TO PRESENT Today, most Americans remain committed to being pioneers in the frontier of space. But some Americans question whether the U.S. government should spend so much money on the space program. They wonder why we should travel to space when there are so many problems on Earth. Supporters of the space program believe that the many benefits from the program are well worth the cost. These benefits include research in medicine and climate.

REACT AND RESPOND Discuss the pros and cons of the space program. What do you think are the practical benefits of space research?

READING 2 The Counter Culture

During the 1960s, the baby boomers became teenagers and young adults. They developed a lifestyle with values that were opposed to those of the traditional culture. It was called the "counter culture." The motto of the counter culture was, "Don't trust anyone over thirty." This article gives you some insight into this stormy period in American history.

The Counter Culture

More than 400,000 people attend the Woodstock Music and Art Fair in 1969.

1   During the 1960s, many young people pursued lifestyles that were different from those of their conservative parents. Some were based on radical politics, while others, such as rural farm communes, developed out of the hippie ideals of love and sharing.

These alternative lifestyles typically had one thing in common: a rejection of the "Establishment."

2   The Establishment was the name given to all symbols of authority, especially the government and parents. Taken together, groups that rejected the Establishment were known as the counter culture. They all hoped to bring about ways of living that were new and better.

3   Perhaps the counter culture's greatest triumph came at the Woodstock Music and Art Fair, held in upstate New York on the weekend of August 15–17, 1969. Four hundred thousand people partied for three days to the music of Jimi Hendrix, Janis Joplin, Santana, and many others. To the rest of the world, the festival looked like a mess, especially after heavy rains turned the concert site into a muddy swamp. When food and medical supplies ran low, the site was declared a disaster area. But the party still went on, people shared what they had, and no one seemed to mind.

CHECK YOUR COMPREHENSION

Answer the questions.

1. What ideas were some of the counter-cultural lifestyles of the 1960s based on?

    a. _____

    b. _____

2. What did the alternative lifestyles have in common?

    _____

3. How does the article define the "Establishment"?

    _____

4. What does the article mention as the counter culture's greatest triumph?

    _____

CULTURE KERNEL

Disco was the most popular form of dance in the 1970s. After the movie Saturday Night Fever *with John Travolta came out, disco began to influence rock music.*

EXPAND YOUR VOCABULARY

Answer the questions.

1. What word in paragraph 1 is an antonym for *liberal*? _____

2. What word in paragraph 1 is an antonym for *urban*? _____

3. What word in paragraph 1 is a synonym for *different*? _____

4. What word in paragraph 2 is an antonym for *accepted*? _____

5. What word in paragraph 3 means *success*? _____

6. What two words in paragraph 3 mean *place*? _____

BUILD YOUR READING SKILLS: Skimming

Skim the newspaper articles about other important events of the 1960s and 1970s. Try to find the general idea of each article. Then match the article with the appropriate headline. Write the correct headline on the line provided.

Watergate Offices Burglarized

Nuclear Disaster Avoided

First Earth Day Celebrated

ARE SOUP CANS ART?

Supreme Court Hands Down Landmark Decision

The World Mourns

1. _____

WASHINGTON, D.C. The sudden death of the young and vigorous American president shocked the world. John F. Kennedy's body was brought back to the White House and placed in the East Room for twenty-four hours. On the Sunday after the assassination, the president's flag-draped coffin was carried to the Capitol Rotunda to lie in state. Throughout the day and night, hundreds of thousands of people filed past the guarded casket.

2. _____

JUNE 18, 1972. Yesterday morning police in Washington, D.C., were called to investigate a burglary at the Democratic Party's National Headquarters in the Watergate complex. They arrested five men, dressed in business suits, who were hiding under desks and behind closed doors. The men were found to be carrying cameras, extra film, and electronic equipment that was obviously intended for wiretapping, sabotage, and other illegal activities.

3. _____

JANUARY 22, 1973. The Supreme Court of the United States has issued its decision in the controversial case of *Roe* v. *Wade*. The court ruled that, except in certain situations, every woman has the right to have an abortion during the first three months of her pregnancy. In effect, this landmark decision has legalized abortion in the United States.

4. _____

The Guggenheim Museum in New York City has just opened the first major pop art (from "popular art") exhibit in the United States. Although pop art is considered outrageous by many, the Guggenheim's decision to hold the show shows the growing respect that the art world is giving to this new kind of art. In fact, critics are already predicting that pop art will be one of the most important artistic movements of the twentieth century. Some of the important paintings include Andy Warhol's *Campbell's Soup Cans* and Roy Lichtenstein's *In the Car*. Pop artists prefer to use images from popular culture for their paintings rather than traditional landscapes or portraits.

5. _____

MARCH 28, 1979. Experts are gathering in Middletown, Pennsylvania, near Harrisburg to try to figure out what caused the fuel rods to overheat at the Three Mile Island nuclear power plant yesterday. The accident occurred at 4 A.M. Indications are that it was the result of human and mechanical error. Scientists and technicians were able to prevent a total core meltdown, so no radioactive isotopes were released outside the power plant. Questions now arise as to the safety of nuclear power.

6. _____

APRIL 22, 1970. More than 20 million people took part today in the first Earth Day. It was the largest organized demonstration in history and quite a success. Some people organized neighborhood clean-ups and planted trees. Others demonstrated against polluters. They brought the issues of air, water, and noise pollution to public attention. In New York City, the mayor closed Fifth Avenue to automobiles, and over 100,000 people attended an ecology fair in Union Square. In response to concerns about the environment, Congress recently passed the Clean Air and Clean Water acts and established strict laws about the use of harmful chemicals. In addition, the government created the Environmental Protection Agency to help control pollution and protect our natural resources.

In the 1970s, as the baby boomers grew older, they became increasingly concerned with their health. This article describes the obsession of many Americans with good food and regular exercise that began in the 1970s.

BEFORE YOU READ

Discuss these questions.

1. Do you try to eat healthy foods? If so, what kinds?

2. How often do you exercise? Do you belong to a gym or health club?

3. What can you learn about a culture by studying the eating habits of the people? What can you learn by studying attitudes toward exercise?

The Health Craze

1   During the 1970s, many people who were frustrated with politics turned inward. The growing environmental movement taught them to be concerned with the health of the Earth, and this concern naturally led them to improve their own health as well.

2   Many Americans began to pay attention to chemical additives in the processed foods they ate as well as the quality of the air they breathed. Whole wheat bread appeared more frequently in supermarkets alongside bleached white breads. Meanwhile, the number of health-food stores multiplied. Many former hippies opened up natural-food restaurants, which served unusually healthful dishes made with tofu, alfalfa sprouts, seaweed, and carob.

3   Americans also began to exercise more. Jogging, in particular, became a popular way of staying in condition while reducing one's risk of heart disease. Sneaker companies made a fortune catering to the footwear and fashion

needs of the new joggers, bikers, and hikers. Even people who did not exercise began to wear running shoes as part of their everyday attire.

Jogging became a popular way of staying in shape in the 1970s.

BUILD YOUR TEST-TAKING SKILLS

Circle the letter of the choice that best completes each sentence.

1. What led people to want to improve their health?
   a. their interest in politics
   b. their concern over the environment
   c. sneaker companies
   d. none of the above

2. The article implies that whole wheat bread has _____.
   a. more chemical additives than bleached white bread
   b. fewer chemical additives than bleached white bread
   c. no chemical additives
   d. more calories than unbleached white bread

3. Natural-food restaurants serve _____.
   a. healthful dishes
   b. food with chemical additives
   c. only dishes made with tofu
   d. sandwiches made on bleached white bread

4. Running shoes became popular with _____.
   a. people who exercised regularly
   b. people who liked jogging
   c. some people who didn't exercise
   d. all of the above

EXPAND YOUR VOCABULARY

Complete each sentence with the correct form of a word from the list.

1. frustrate, frustrated, frustrating, frustration
   a. The little boy kicked the door in _____.
   b. Don't get _____. It takes time to learn a language.
   c. They keep sending me the wrong form; it's very _____.
   d. It _____ me when the train is late.

2. political, politically, politics, politician
   a. My brother has never been interested in _____.
   b. He is not very _____.
   c. Unfortunately, _____ are often not trusted.
   d. Many people today are very _____ aware.

3. process, procession, processor

   a. The high school band marched down Main Street in a long
      _____.

   b. My father wants to get my mother a food _____ for her
      birthday.

   c. Your application is being _____.

4. multiply, multiplication, multiple

   a. The company's problems have _____ during the last year.

   b. _____ choice tests are usually very difficult.

   c. The _____ of white blood cells indicates infection.

BUILD YOUR SKILLS: Paraphrasing

Paraphrase these sentences from Reading 3.

1. Jogging, in particular, became a popular way of staying in condition while
   reducing one's risk of heart disease.

   _____

   _____

2. The growing environmental movement taught people to be concerned with
   the health of the Earth, and this concern led them to improve their own
   health as well.

   _____

   _____

3. Many Americans began to pay attention to the chemical additives in the
   processed foods they ate as well as the quality of the air they breathed.

   _____

   _____

4. Sneaker companies made a fortune catering to the footwear and fashion
   needs of the new joggers, bikers, and hikers.

   _____

   _____

WRITE ABOUT IT

Design a survey to find out about the eating, exercise, and health habits of people in the community you are living in now. Write your questions on the lines. Interview at least five people.

Example: On the average, how many hours a week do you exercise?

1. _____

2. _____

3. _____

4. _____

5. _____

6. _____

7. _____

8. _____

TALK ABOUT IT

Discuss the results of your survey with your classmates.

 LINKING PAST TO PRESENT Since the United States is such a diverse country, it is impossible to make a generalization about the eating habits of its residents. The diet of some Americans consists of fast foods such as hamburgers and french fries. Many Americans also eat a lot of "junk food" such as candy and potato chips that have a lot of fat and sugar but little nutritional value. On the other hand, many Americans are very concerned about what they eat. They try to choose foods that are lower in fat and sugar and higher in protein, vitamins, and fiber. They prefer fresh foods rather than canned or frozen foods and watch the number of calories they eat.

REACT AND RESPOND What is your impression of the eating habits of the Americans you know? How would you describe the eating habits of the people in your country? In general, do you think people in your country are concerned with the health value of what they eat?

Technological change was another characteristic of the 1970s. In the early 1900s, the automobile changed the way Americans lived. Then radio and TV came along and transformed their lives again. Since the 1970s, the greatest cause of change has been the computer. This article traces the development of the computer industry through recent decades.

Computers

1   Computers have revolutionized the way people study, work, do business, entertain themselves, and organize their lives. In the mid-1940s, computers were the size of houses and as expensive as airplanes. They were also difficult to use and didn't have the power of modern computers. The development of the transistor in the 1950s resulted in faster, smaller, and more reliable computers, which then became more widely used in business. In the 1970s, the personal computer was developed, and soon the average person could buy and use computers.

2   In 1976, two young friends with an entrepreneurial spirit had an idea. Steve Wozniak and Steve Jobs designed and built the first small, inexpensive personal computer. They called it the Apple I. They sold 600 units of their Apple I for $666 apiece, mainly to hobbyists and electronics lovers. This was the start of Apple Computer, Incorporated. Working out of the Jobs's family garage, the two Steves developed the Apple II in 1977. It was one of the first PCs to incorporate color graphics and a keyboard. The Apple II, which sold for $1,195, was a huge success. It holds a special place in the history of computer use because it was the first truly successful, easy-to-use, general-purpose personal computer.

3   The Apple II soon began turning up in business offices as well as homes across the country. Within ten years, millions of average Americans became computer literate and were using PCs both at work and at home. Today, these machines affect almost every aspect of American life. Schools, hospitals, and businesses all rely on computers to process information and keep records.

Computers have revolutionized today's world

CHECK YOUR COMPREHENSION

*Based on information in Reading 4, mark each of the statements true (**T**) or false (**F**). However, if the article doesn't give you enough information to determine if a statement is true or false, write a **?** on the line.*

_____ 1. Steve Wozniak and Steve Jobs were both engineers.

_____ 2. The Apple II was easier to use than the Apple I.

_____ 3. Computers in the mid-1940s were small and affordable.

_____ 4. The first computer was built in the 1930s.

_____ 5. The development of the PC allowed the average person to use computers.

_____ 6. Bigger computers always have more power than smaller computers.

_____ 7. The Apple II cost less than the Apple I.

_____ 8. Apple Computer, Incorporated, was the most successful computer company in the 1980s.

CULTURE KERNEL

The computing power of today's simple digital wristwatches is greater than that of ENIAC, the world's first electronic computer.[2]

LINKING PAST TO PRESENT   A lot has happened since the first personal computer came out in 1977. Today, it is clear that personal computers have revolutionized our homes and offices. In 1995, 37 percent of American households had at least one computer. That number is rapidly increasing as more and more people are buying personal computers. In 1999, almost as many PCs were sold as TVs.

REACT AND RESPOND   Discuss the ways that computers directly affect your life. Consider, for example, word processing, electronic mailing, banking, shopping, fighting crime, using a library, playing games, or keeping medical information.

READING 5   The Long Battle for Women's Equality

This article is long and looks very challenging at first. However, since it reviews of a lot of information you have already studied, it will not be as difficult as you may think. You will recognize some of the themes and terms in this article because you have read about them in other articles in this book. Previewing before you read will give you a general idea of what the article is about.

---

[2]"Seeing the Century," *American Heritage,* December 1999: 61.

BUILD YOUR READING SKILLS: Previewing

Preview the article by following these steps.

1. Look at the title of the article and write it on the line. What do you think this article will be about?

    _____

    _____

2. Read the subtitle and write it on the line. What do you think the main idea of this article might be?

    _____

    _____

3. Write the headings on the lines and predict what you think the section will be about.

    a. _____

    _____

    b. _____

    _____

    c. _____

    _____

    d. _____

    _____

    e. _____

    _____

    f. _____

    _____

    g. _____

    _____

    h. _____

    _____

4. Read the first and last paragraphs of the article.

5. Reading 5 contains one picture. Guess why the author included this picture.

6. Read the first sentence of each paragraph.

7. Now read the article one time all the way through. Do not stop to look up words in the dictionary and do not worry about parts that you do not understand. The purpose of the first reading is simply to give you a general sense of the article and to prepare you for a more careful reading.

The Long Battle for Women's Equality

By Tamar Rothenberg

Why Did U.S. Women Wait 144 Years Before They Gained the Right to Vote?

Women fight for equality.

1   The pioneer spirit of colonial America did much to change attitudes about the role of women. The settlers' main concern was survival—collecting or growing food, building shelter, and protecting themselves. On the frontier, marriage was a close economic partnership. Men did the field work, the hunting, and the fishing. Women did the housework, took care of children, prepared the food. In towns, shopkeepers were usually assisted by their wives, who often took over when their husbands died.

2   Economic changes toward the mid-1800s changed the way Americans viewed work and had a major effect on women. As factories opened, "real work" began to be defined as paid labor performed outside the home. Gradually, some women began to take jobs outside their homes. They taught school, nursed the sick, and worked in knitting mills. Communities sometimes preferred to hire women teachers because they could be paid less than men teachers. Women who tried to move into "men's" occupations were often ridiculed.

SEPARATE ROLES FOR MEN AND WOMEN

3   Throughout the 1800s, most Americans felt that men and women belonged to separate areas in life. The man's area was the rough, competitive world of politics, business, and public activity. A woman's place was in the home, where her role was the moral guardian and "civilizer of mankind."

4   For poor women, however, there was little time for leisure. Women, especially immigrants, were given the worst jobs, and they worked an average of twelve hours a day for very small wages. For black women in slavery, physical and sexual abuse often added to their hardships.

SOCIETY'S MORAL GUARDIANS

5   The idea of women's role as the "moral guardians" of society encouraged some to join the movement to abolish slavery in the 1830s. But many antislavery activists, known as abolitionists, couldn't accept women taking public action on a national issue. In spite of this attitude, abolitionist Lucretia Mott formed the first

(continues on next page)

woman's antislavery society in Philadelphia, Pennsylvania, in 1833. A decade later, Mott played a leading role in the birth of the women's rights movement.

6   In 1840, Mott was among a group of women abolitionists who were denied seats at an antislavery convention in London, England. Mott discussed her frustration with Elizabeth Cady Stanton, who had also traveled to London. Mott and Stanton decided to fight for women's liberation as well as that of black slaves.

WOMEN ORGANIZE

7   Mott and Stanton organized a women's rights convention in Seneca Falls, New York, in July 1848. The convention adopted a Declaration of Sentiments, modeled after the Declaration of Independence. In it, women demanded their "inalienable rights" as U.S. citizens. Around the country, reaction to the Seneca Falls declaration ranged from outrage to amusement. Some people called it "the most shocking and unnatural incident ever recorded in the history of womanity." Others laughed at this "petticoat rebellion." But Stanton declared the event "a great success."

8   By the time the Civil War began in 1861, several states had enacted laws giving married women some control of their own property. The war brought a temporary halt to the women's rights struggle, as women joined the war effort.

THE FOURTEENTH AMENDMENT: WOMEN EXCLUDED

9   During the war, Elizabeth Cady Stanton and other leading feminists—including Susan B. Anthony—helped win approval for the Thirteenth Amendment,

which ended slavery. Then they asked that women be included in the Fourteenth Amendment, which guaranteed black males' citizenship and civil rights, including the right to vote. But many abolitionist leaders, including strong defenders of women's rights such as Frederick Douglass, told them to wait. They said that adding women's rights to the amendment would make it harder to pass. Other abolitionists spoke out for the right of women to vote. One outspoken leader for universal suffrage, expanding the right to vote to all citizens, black and white, male and female, was ex-slave Sojourner Truth.

STRIDES IN EDUCATION

10   Women did not need the vote to improve the education they received. Here, the leader was Emma Willard, a teacher and educational reformer. Willard believed that educated women would be better wives and mothers. Oberlin College (Ohio) became the first college to admit women in 1833. In 1837, Mount Holyoke (Massachusetts) became the first women's college.

11   By the late 1800s, many women had taken on the role of moral guardian to the nation's public life. Women were leaders in the movement to abolish the sale of liquor and in prison and mental institution reform. Career-minded women often went into social work. The most famous social reformer of the time was Jane Addams, who founded one of the nation's first settlement houses. Called Hull House, it was located in a Chicago slum and provided services to the poor. Settlement workers such as Addams did more than help the urban poor. They also fought for public health and housing laws and for an end to child labor.

The Susan B. Anthony Amendment

12   In 1878, U.S. Senator A. A. Sargent of California introduced a proposed amendment that would give women the right to vote. The proposal was referred to as the "Susan B. Anthony Amendment." Sargent's bill did not pass, but it was introduced in Congress almost every year for the next forty years.

13   That same year, Elizabeth Cady Stanton's daughter, Harriet Stanton Blatch, helped organize the first women's suffrage parade in New York City. Pictures of marching women in long white dresses became the symbol of the women's rights struggle. In Washington, D.C., 5,000 suffragists made front-page news in 1913 by marching the day before Woodrow Wilson's inauguration as U.S. president.

Ratification at Last

14   Congress finally passed the Susan B. Anthony Amendment in 1919. A year later, the states ratified it as the Nineteenth Amendment to the Constitution.

15   For most Americans, the 1920s were a time of changing lifestyles. Many homemakers now bought their bread from bakeries and purchased ready-made clothing from department stores. By 1929, almost 70 percent of U.S. homes had electricity, which powered many kinds of labor-saving appliances.

16   Two new images of women seemed to typify the era. One was the "flapper," who wore short skirts, smoked cigarettes, and used makeup. The other was the "working girl." Unmarried young women entered the workforce, taking over many jobs once held by men. By 1925, 8.5 million women worked outside the home.

17   Still, most people disapproved of married women who worked—even during the Great Depression of the 1930s. "I would rather turn on the gas and put an end to the whole family than let my wife support me," one unemployed husband said. Despite such attitudes, U.S. entry into World War II in 1941 sent millions of women into the workforce to replace the men who went to war. When the war ended in 1945, however, most women returned to their homes.

18   After the hardships of the Depression and war, both women and men turned to the stability of the family. Many women quit their jobs and returned to homemaking. By 1959, half of all women were getting married by age twenty. The percentage of women in college actually dropped between 1940 and 1960.

The Equal Rights Amendment

19   "The image of the American woman as a changing, growing individual in a changing world was shattered. . . . Her limitless world shrunk to the cozy walls of home," wrote Betty Friedan in her 1963 book, *The Feminine Mystique*. Friedan argued that women needed to form identities apart from their roles as wives and mothers.

20   In 1966, Friedan helped found the National Organization for Women (NOW) to push for laws strengthening women's rights and interests. NOW's top priority was the proposed Equal Rights Amendment (ERA). Many people were opposed to the ERA because they felt it would remove laws protecting women and that it would destroy the traditional family. Congress passed the ERA in 1972, but the amendment won approval in only

(continues on next page)

35 states—3 less than it needed to become law.

21   Today, the struggle to improve the position of women in society continues. More people are recognizing that history is only half told without women's side of the story.

CHECK YOUR COMPREHENSION

A. *Mark each item true (T) or false (F).*

_____ **1.** The pioneer spirit helped change society's attitude about the role of women.

_____ **2.** Economic changes in the mid-1800s led to an increase in the number of women working outside their homes.

_____ **3.** Throughout the nineteenth century, most Americans believed that men and women belonged to different areas in life.

_____ **4.** Most Americans supported the goals of the Seneca Falls Convention.

_____ **5.** The women's rights struggle made great advances during the Civil War.

_____ **6.** By the beginning of the twentieth century, most people approved of married women who worked.

_____ **7.** The struggle to improve the position of women continues today.

B. *Match each name from the reading with an accomplishment.*

_____ **1.** Susan B. Anthony

_____ **2.** Harriet S. Blatch

_____ **3.** Betty Friedan

_____ **4.** Elizabeth Cady Stanton

_____ **5.** Emma Willard

a. social reformer who founded Hull House

b. formed the first women's antislavery society; played important role in birth of women's rights movement

c. with Stanton, helped win approval for Thirteenth Amendment

d. author of *The Feminine Mystique*; helped found NOW

e. ex-slave, leader for universal suffrage

_____ **6.** Jane Addams

f. helped organize first woman's suffrage parade in New York

_____ **7.** Lucretia Mott

g. leader in educational reform for women

_____ **8.** Sojourner Truth

h. helped organize Seneca Falls Convention with Lucretia Mott

BUILD YOUR READING SKILLS: Using Context to Understand Vocabulary

Using clues such as punctuation, grammar, and the general meaning of the sentence, try to figure out the meaning of the words in bold type. Write an approximate definition or synonym of the word in bold. Do not use your dictionary.

1. The settlers' main concern was **survival**—collecting or growing food, building shelter, and protecting themselves.

_____

2. But many antislavery activists, known as **abolitionists**, couldn't accept women taking public action on a national issue.

_____

3. By the time the Civil War began in 1861, several states had **enacted** laws giving married women some control of their own property.

_____

4. One outspoken leader for universal **suffrage**, expanding the right to vote to all citizens, black and white, male and female, was ex-slave Sojourner Truth.

_____

LINKING PAST TO PRESENT The women's movement has proved to be an enduring aspect of American society. By the late 1970s, the women's movement was attracting women of all ages, ethnic backgrounds, and classes. The National Organization for Women was established in 1966, and by 1977 it had 65,000 members. This number has increased to 500,000 today, and the women's movement continues to gain strength.

REACT AND RESPOND Discuss the role of women in your country. Has there been a "women's rights" movement? In what ways do women influence the economy, religion, education, medicine, or politics?

HISTORY MAKER: César Chávez

Read the list of facts about César Chávez, an important Mexican-American labor leader. Then choose the information you want from the list to write a paragraph about him on a separate piece of paper. Be sure to begin your paragraph with a topic sentence that states the main idea. Include transition words to guide the reader from one point to the next.

César Chávez, Mexican-American labor leader

- founded and led the first successful farm workers' union in U.S. history

- born in Yuma, Arizona, in 1927. Died in 1993

- raised in migrant worker camps

- left school after the sixth grade

- served in the U.S. Navy during World War II

- organized farm workers into the United Farm Workers (UFW)

- organized nationwide boycotts of grapes, wine, and lettuce to pressure California growers to sign contracts with UFW

- influenced by Mohandas Gandhi and Martin Luther King Jr.

- believed in nonviolence practiced by Gandhi and King (strikes, fasts, marches)

- conducted twenty-five-day fast in 1968 to reaffirm the UFW's commitment to nonviolence

- called by Senator Robert F. Kennedy "one of the heroic figures of our time"

- didn't eat for thirty-six days in 1988 to protest use of pesticides

- received the Presidential Medal of Freedom in 1994

Exchange paragraphs with a partner. Read your partner's paragraph and check it for correct grammar, punctuation, and capitalization.

SKILL REVIEW: Understanding Transitions

Read the passage about credit cards and underline the transitions. In the margin, identify the type of relationship the transitions signify.

Credit Cards

1   By the 1960s, the "buy now–pay later" concept of buying on credit had been part of the American culture for many years. Buying on credit meant that people could spend more money than they actually had. In 1950, Frank MacNamara and Ralph Schneider introduced the first credit card. They called their card the Diner's Club because people could use it to charge food and drinks at twenty-eight restaurants in New York City. At that time, the use of credit cards was limited. What was really revolutionary about MacNamara and Schneider's idea was that it allowed people to use only one credit card in many different locations and then pay with one monthly bill. The idea caught on quickly because of its convenience to consumers and profitability to businesses. American Express and Bank Americard were the next to offer this new type of card that could be used in many places to buy almost anything. Today, 80 percent of all Americans have at least one credit card. From the start, there have been negative and positive predictions as to how the credit card would change society. There was and still is concern about the distribution of cards to those who cannot afford to pay their bills. In addition, card loss, theft, and fraud have always been problems. On the other hand, credit cards encourage spending, and that is good for the economy. Also, some experts have predicted that credit cards will turn us eventually into a cashless society. If that happens, it would mean a dramatic reduction in violent crime, since 75 percent of all crime is motivated by the need for cash.

PUT IT TOGETHER

Discuss the questions.

1. How has the role of women changed in your country over the past fifty years?

2. In her book, *The Feminine Mystique,* Betty Friedan argued that women need to "reassert themselves and establish identities apart from their roles as wives and mothers." Do you agree or disagree with Friedan? Why?

3. How dependent are you, directly or indirectly, on computers?

4. Much of the discontent associated with the 1960s and 1970s was related to controversy over the involvement of the United States in the Vietnam War. Do you think that countries should become involved in the political conflicts of other countries?

THE END OF A CENTURY

1980–2000

*I*n this chapter, you will examine the technological, environmental, and population trends that characterized the end of the twentieth century.

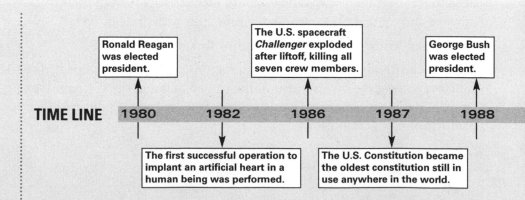

MAKE A CONNECTION

What has been happening in your country since 1980?

TIME LINE

| 1980 | 1982 | 1986 | 1987 | 1988 |

Ronald Reagan was elected president.

The U.S. spacecraft *Challenger* exploded after liftoff, killing all seven crew members.

George Bush was elected president.

The first successful operation to implant an artificial heart in a human being was performed.

The U.S. Constitution became the oldest constitution still in use anywhere in the world.

The United States at the End of the Twentieth Century

Among other things, the 1980s and 1990s were marked by technological advances, changes in population, and continuing concern about the environment.

The Technology Revolution

By the end of the century, advances in technology revolutionized almost every aspect of life. Personal computers, cellular phones, beepers, fax machines, electronic mail, and the Internet all affected American society in some way. These technologies changed the way people communicate, study, diagnose and cure disease, fight crime, entertain themselves, shop, work, and vacation. Although the end of the century was a time of prosperity for many Americans, it was also a time when the gap between the rich and the poor got wider. Many less fortunate Americans were left out of the information revolution.

A New Wave of Immigrants

The composition of the U.S. population changed dramatically toward the end of the century. This was due, in part, to a great increase in immigration. The new wave of immigrants, numbering approximately 9 million, came mostly from Asian and Hispanic countries. Just like their counterparts from Europe a hundred years ago, these new arrivals influenced the music, art, food, fashion,

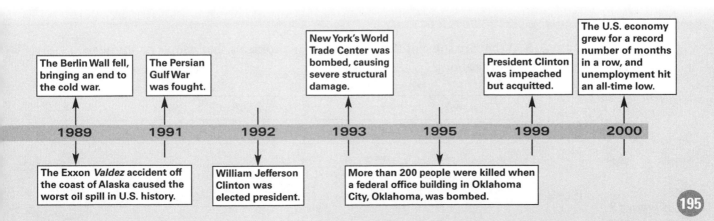

1989 — The Berlin Wall fell, bringing an end to the cold war.

The Exxon *Valdez* accident off the coast of Alaska caused the worst oil spill in U.S. history.

1991 — The Persian Gulf War was fought.

1992 — William Jefferson Clinton was elected president.

1993 — New York's World Trade Center was bombed, causing severe structural damage.

1995 — More than 200 people were killed when a federal office building in Oklahoma City, Oklahoma, was bombed.

1999 — President Clinton was impeached but acquitted.

2000 — The U.S. economy grew for a record number of months in a row, and unemployment hit an all-time low.

voting patterns, and economy of the country. During this time, the number of mixed marriages also increased. More and more people began marrying outside of their ethnic, racial, and religious group. As a result, there is a growing pool of young Americans who are ethnically mixed.

The Continuing Civil Rights Struggle

During the 1980s and 1990s, minority groups across the nation worked hard to receive an equal share of their civil rights. Women, African Americans, Hispanics, Native Americans, Asian Americans, gay men and women, and people with disabilities all made significant strides. However, despite these efforts, tensions between people of different races and different ethnic backgrounds remained high.

A Fragile Planet

As the century drew to a close, more people became concerned about our fragile planet. The environmental movement grew stronger as people worried about destruction of the Earth's natural resources, global warming, and pollution. Although the environmental movement made important gains, these environmental problems still threatened the planet.

As the twenty-first century begins, globalization is making the world a smaller place by bringing nations more closely together economically, politically, and socially. In the years to come, we can hope that solutions to the problems of the United States and the world will come from countries working together, striving for a better life for all.

Answer the questions.

1. How has the new technology changed American society?

   _____

   _____

2. How did the new wave of immigrants influence American society?

   _____

   _____

3. What are some of the environmental problems that people continue to worry about?

   _____

   _____

   _____

Technological advances of the 1980s and 1990s have influenced the way we think, work, and play. The Internet is one of the most significant of these technological advances. It connects millions of people around the world to each other and allows them to share information almost instantaneously. This article explores some of the issues involved in getting everyone hooked up to the Internet.

BEFORE YOU READ

Discuss these questions with your classmates.

1. Have you ever used the Internet?

2. Read the four headings in the article. Write them on the lines below and guess what the article will be about.

   a. _____

   b. _____

   c. _____

   d. _____

CULTURE KERNEL

America's 82 million baby boomers pursued counter-cultural lifestyles in the 1960s. By the 1990s, they were no longer antiestablishment. They played the stock market, pouring money into investments for their approaching retirement.

Getting Wired

The Struggle to Bring All Americans into the Computer Age

1   On March 12, 1933, President Franklin D. Roosevelt gave his first "fireside chat" over the radio. He discussed the topics and events that mattered most to Americans. Though earlier presidents had spoken on the radio, FDR was the first to use this technology to connect with the American people and explain his ideas to them.

2   Flash-forward sixty-six years: A new technology, the Internet, had become widely available. Recently President Bill Clinton held his first "cyberchat." Computer users across the United States asked him questions online.

(continues on next page)

THE INTERNET TAKES OFF

3   Clinton's chat illustrates how far technology came during the twentieth century. In the 1990s alone, computers went from mainly storing and analyzing information to also sending and receiving it on a giant scale. Through the Internet, millions of people around the world share information and ideas. During Clinton's two terms in office, the number of computers connected to the Internet skyrocketed from 1.3 million to more than 56 million worldwide.

4   Even so, plenty of Americans have been left out of the information revolution. Those who don't have enough money for a computer or who live in rural areas, far from public libraries, can't learn to use the Internet or gain other computer skills. In his cyberchat, Clinton emphasized the importance of "unleashing the power of information technology" and making computers available to everyone.

A TROUBLING GAP

5   The gap between the computer rich and the computer poor is the focus of a report from the U.S. Commerce Department called "Falling through the Net: Defining the Digital Divide." The report says that families with incomes higher than $75,000 a year are nine times as likely to have a computer as those with low incomes. Richer families are twenty times as likely to have Internet access.

6   The difference exists in schools, too. Just 16 percent of classrooms in poor, largely African-American and Hispanic communities have Internet access. Compare that with 80 percent in wealthy neighborhoods.

NETTING FUTURE JOBS

7   Computer technology in the 1990s opened a floodgate of information. A lot of that information is available on the World Wide Web, the giant piece of the Internet that is made up of "sites" run by individuals and companies. In 1993, there were just 130 websites. In 1999, there were more than 3.6 million, on nearly every topic, from aardvarks to zippers!

8   With dozens of new websites popping up every day, the number of job opportunities for people with Web skills is growing quickly, too. In the near future, says the Commerce Department, 60 percent of all U.S. jobs will require technological skills.

9   That's bad news for kids who don't have access to computers at home or in the classroom. How will they gain computer skills? The good news: Many new programs are under way to make sure that everyone has a fair shot at being part of the digital revolution.

EQUAL ACCESS FOR ALL

10   Recently, America Online, which brings the Internet to more people than any other company, announced a generous new program. AOL joined with several other groups to give millions of dollars in free computers, software, and technology tutoring to poor children. The $10 million program, PowerUp, will be offered in schools and community centers nationwide.

11   Other programs serve local communities. In California's Silicon Valley, home to many high-tech companies, a group called Plugged In is training kids who might otherwise miss out on computer education. High school students from poor

neighborhoods around Palo Alto can attend a free ten-week course that teaches them how to create websites. Computers are donated by big companies like IBM.

12   After completing the program, teens get a chance to use their new skills to earn money by creating sites for local companies. The money is nice, says Omar Ortiz, sixteen. But he insists he'd work for free: "Any computer skill I learn here is priceless."

BUILD YOUR READING SKILLS: Recognizing Main Ideas

Describe the main idea of each section in your own words.

The Internet Takes Off: _____

_____

_____

A Troubling Gap: _____

_____

_____

Netting Future Jobs: _____

_____

_____

Equal Access for All: _____

_____

_____

BUILD YOUR TEST-TAKING SKILLS

Circle the letter of the choice that best completes each statement or answers the question.

1. The article mainly discusses _____.
   a. Roosevelt's fireside chats
   b. Clinton's views on the Internet
   c. how the Internet works
   d. unequal access to the Internet

2. According to the article, _____.
   a. not all Americans are part of the computer revolution
   b. most Americans are part of the computer revolution
   c. adults need to use the Internet more than children
   d. all Americans have equal access to the Internet

3. Which of the following is a conclusion you can make based on the article?
   a. Only wealthy people should have access to the Internet.
   b. Schools should not use the Internet as a teaching tool.
   c. It is important for all Americans to have equal access to the Internet.
   d. The Internet will become less important in the future.

4. Where does the author describe the program Plugged In?
   a. Paragraph 2   **c.** Paragraph 8
   b. Paragraph 6   **d.** Paragraph 11

5. Where does the author discuss the number of computers connected to the Internet?
   a. Paragraph 1   **c.** Paragraph 9
   b. Paragraph 3   **d.** Paragraph 11

6. The phrase *is made up of* in the second sentence of paragraph 7 means
_____.

   a. consists of   **c.** agreed with
   b. excluded from   **d.** paid by

BUILD YOUR READING SKILLS: Examining Meaning

Read each sentence and circle the letter of the sentence that is closest in meaning.

1. Though earlier presidents had spoken on the radio, FDR was the first to use this technology to connect with the American people and explain his ideas to them.
   a. FDR was the first president to speak on the radio.
   b. FDR wasn't the first president to speak on the radio, but he was the first to use radio to explain his ideas to the people.
   c. Like earlier presidents, FDR used radio to explain his ideas to the people.

2. Clinton's chat illustrates how far technology came during the twentieth century.
   a. Clinton's use of the Internet to connect with the people shows how much technology has advanced.
   b. Clinton's use of the Internet shows how much still needs to be done.
   c. Clinton's chat is an example of how confusing technology has become.

3. Richer families are twenty times as likely to have Internet access.
   a. Richer families like to have Internet access twenty times a month.
   b. Richer families like to use the Internet twenty times more than other families.
   c. Richer families have twenty times as much of a chance to have Internet access.

4. A group called Plugged In is training kids who might otherwise miss out on computer education.
   a. Plugged In gives computer education to all children.
   b. Without Plugged In, some students might not get computer education.
   c. A group of kids missed out on calling Plugged In.

EXPAND YOUR VOCABULARY

Circle the letter of the word that is closest in meaning to the word in bold type.

1. Clinton's **chat** illustrates how far technology came during the twentieth century.
   a. article   b. talk   c. computer

2. In the 1990s alone, computers went from mainly storing and analyzing information to also sending and receiving it on a **giant** scale.
   a. huge   b. average   c. small

3. During Clinton's two terms in office, the number of computers connected to the Internet **skyrocketed** from 1.3 million to more than 56 million worldwide.
   a. greatly increased   b. slightly increased   c. doubled

4. Even so, **plenty of** Americans have been **left out of** the information revolution.

   plenty of
   a. few   b. some   c. many

   left out of
   a. excluded from   b. included in   c. afraid of

5. Clinton **emphasized** the importance of "unleashing the power of information technology" and making computers available to everyone.
   a. guessed   **b.** stressed   **c.** blessed

6. The gap between the computer rich and the computer poor is the **focus** of a report from the U.S. Commerce Department.
   a. main point   **b.** detail   **c.** conclusion

7. Compare that with 80 percent in **wealthy** neighborhoods.
   a. rich   **b.** new   **c.** old

8. With dozens of new websites **popping up** every day, the number of job opportunities for people with Web skills is growing quickly, too.
   a. exploding   **b.** decreasing   **c.** appearing

9. The good news: Many new programs are under way to make sure that everyone has a **fair shot** at being part of the digital revolution.
   a. good aim   **b.** equal chance   **c.** unfair advantage

10. "Any computer skill I learn here is **priceless**."
    a. very valuable   **b.** inexpensive   **c.** without value

---

 LINKING PAST TO PRESENT In the 1980s and 1990s, technology revolutionized every aspect of life. Many people, however, question whether technology has made life simpler or more complex for the average person. Some people are happy that they do not have to be in their office to work. Technology has made it so easy for them to keep in touch that they can work from home. But others claim that technology has increased their stress level. They don't like the hundreds of e-mails, phone calls, and faxes they have to send and respond to every day. They complain that technology has given us the tools for improved communication, but none of it is face to face.

REACT AND RESPOND Do you feel that technology pulls people apart or brings them together? Have the recent changes in technology made your life simpler or more complex?

TALK ABOUT IT

Look at the cartoon. Do you think it is funny? Why or why not?

Do your laptop and fax machine accompany you on vacation?

READING 2   **From Soda Bottles to Sweaters**

In the 1980s and 1990s, new types of clothes were designed in response to the concerns of many Americans to keep fit and protect the environment. Some clothing companies, such as the one described in this article, made a commitment to manufacturing products that do not harm the environment.

BEFORE YOU READ

Discuss these questions with your classmates.

1. Is sports clothing a big industry in your country?

2. When you shop for clothing, do you pay more attention to price, quality, style, comfort, or fabric?

3. Use your imagination to guess what the title of this article means. What do you think the article will be about?

From Soda Bottles to Sweaters

1   Yvon Chouinard loves the outdoors. He surfs, climbs rocks, skis, hikes, kayaks, and runs Patagonia, a multimillion-dollar company. Although Mr. Chouinard does all of these things very well, his real passion is saving the Earth. In fact, Mr. Chouinard says he had two reasons for starting his company. First, he wanted to earn enough money so he could become an active environmental philanthropist. Second, he wanted the freedom to spend as much time as possible enjoying nature.

2   Patagonia designs and distributes clothing for use in extreme outdoor weather conditions. It originally started in the 1960s as a climbing and mountaineering equipment company. Yvon Chouinard used to manufacture climbing hardware and sold it out of the back of his car up in the mountains. He then moved on to selling clothing for use in the mountains. All of his products continue to be designed for comfort, simplicity, and versatility.

3   Mr. Chouinard's business grew rapidly, and by the late 1990s, its sales had reached $180 million. Patagonia's clothing is popular because it is versatile, comfortable, dries quickly, and remains warm even when it is wet. It works well in hot, cold, wet, dry, humid, arid, windy, and calm weather. Patagonia products are sold around the world through its mail-order catalog. It also does a lot of business over the Internet.

4   In addition to its commitment to providing high-quality products to its customers, Patagonia is also committed to the environment. It pledges 1 percent of its sales each year to the preservation and restoration of the natural environment. With recent annual sales of $180 million, the company gave $1.8 million to environmental groups around the world.

5   In the early 1990s, Patagonia acknowledged in its catalog that every product Patagonia designed and distributed polluted the Earth in some way. The company decided to decrease the impact of its products on the environment and to help people learn more about environmental problems. As a result, in the fall of 1993, Patagonia introduced a new product, a sweater made of recycled soda bottles! The warm, soft, fuzzy fabric was called PCR® (Post-Consumer Recycled) Synchilla®. (*Post-consumer recycled* refers to products that have been used by people before.) Because soda bottles are made from very high-quality plastic, it is possible to melt the bottles and make them into yarn for clothes.

6   It takes twenty-five two-liter bottles to make each sweater. The result is that for each sweater made, twenty-five fewer soda bottles go into a landfill somewhere. In addition, it takes less energy and fewer natural resources to make PCR® Synchilla® than it does to make virgin (new) polyester. The first sweaters were made of 80 percent PCR® Synchilla® and 20 percent virgin polyester. Within a year, the technology had improved, and the ratio became 90 percent PCR® Synchilla® and 10 percent virgin polyester in some products. This meant that more soda bottles were needed to produce an item,

so fewer bottles went into landfills. Patagonia's PCR® Synchilla® products help people see and understand the positive results of recycling. In fact, Patagonia was so determined to share this new technology that it did not patent the process. It hopes that other companies will also use it.

7   In addition to innovations in the technology of making fabrics, Patagonia has also been urging people to simplify their lives and recycle clothes they don't need. The company tries to make the products as multifunctional as possible. For example, rather than having one pair of shorts to play volleyball in and four other pairs for basketball, kayaking, hiking, and running, Patagonia offers one pair which can be used in a variety of sports under a variety of conditions. This means more space in your closet and less trash in the landfill.

8   Patagonia is committed to sharing the issue of environmental responsibility with other businesses. Mr. Chouinard, the board of directors, and the employees think of the company as a tool for social change. It is their hope that more companies will recognize the environmental "costs" of doing business and try to be more planet-friendly.

BUILD YOUR READING SKILLS: Recognizing Main Ideas

A. *Read the list of main points from Reading 2. Write the number of the paragraph that discusses each point.*

_____ **1.** Patagonia's commitment to designing multifunctional clothing

_____ **2.** Patagonia's financial commitment to restoration and preservation of the environment

_____ **3.** how the company got started

_____ **4.** the introduction of a sweater made from recycled soda bottles

_____ **5.** information about the company's founder

_____ **6.** why Patagonia clothing is popular

_____ **7.** how Patagonia's new technology for making sweaters helps the environment

CULTURE KERNEL

The average American generates twenty-five tons of waste for landfills every year.

B. *Match each cause with its result.*

_____ 1. Patagonia wanted to decrease the impact of its products on the environment.

_____ 2. Patagonia wants people to simplify their lives.

_____ 3. It takes twenty-five two-liter bottles to make each PCR® Synchilla® sweater.

_____ 4. Patagonia's clothes are comfortable and versatile.

_____ 5. Patagonia didn't patent its new technology.

_____ 6. Patagonia improved the process for making PCR® Synchilla®.

_____ 7. Patagonia is committed to the environment.

a. Patagonia pledges 1 percent of its annual sales to environmental causes.

b. Patagonia clothing is popular.

c. Patagonia developed PCR® Synchilla® to make sweaters.

d. Fewer bottles go into landfills.

e. Patagonia makes multifunctional clothes.

f. Other companies will be able to use the new technology.

g. The new ratio for PCR® Synchilla® is nine to one.

CHECK YOUR COMPREHENSION

Check the statements that are true about Patagonia.

_____ 1. It designs high-fashion formal clothes.

_____ 2. It sells products through a mail-order catalog and the Internet.

_____ 3. It tried to keep the new technology from competitors.

_____ 4. It designs different types of clothes for each sport in order to sell more products.

_____ 5. It believes in the positive results of recycling.

_____ 6. Its products are comfortable, versatile, and simple.

EXPAND YOUR VOCABULARY

A. *Decide whether the pairs of words are synonyms or antonyms. If they are synonyms, circle* **S.** *If they are antonyms, circle* **A.**

1. versatile	multifunctional	S	A
2. humid	arid	S	A
3. pledge	promise	S	A
4. impact	effect	S	A
5. recognize	realize	S	A
6. ratio	proportion	S	A
7. committed	dedicated	S	A

B. *Answer the questions.*

1. What word in paragraph 1 means someone who gives a lot of money to charity? _____

2. What phrase in paragraph 2 is used to describe something that was true in the past, but is not true now? _____

3. In paragraph 3, the word _____ is a synonym for the word *quickly*.

4. What word in paragraph 3 means *having many different uses*? _____

5. What word in paragraph 3 means *dry*? _____

6. In paragraph 4, which word is the antonym of *destruction*? _____

7. In paragraph 7, the word _____ refers to the introduction of new ideas or methods.

8. In paragraph 7, which word means *to encourage* or *strongly suggest*? _____

9. What prefix is used in words in paragraphs 1 and 7 to mean *many*? _____

TALK ABOUT IT

Are you concerned about the environment? What do you personally do to protect the environment? Make a list and compare it with those of your classmates.

_____ _____

_____ _____

_____ _____

READING 3 The Changing Face of America

The United States continues to be a heterogeneous society. Americans are composed of many ethnic, racial, and religious groups. In the past, members of the same group tended to stick together and usually married within the group. Today, this trend is changing. More and more members of one ethnic, racial, or religious group are marrying outside of their community. In this article, you will read about the growing number of children in mixed-race families.

The Changing Face of America

1   Tiger Woods has been called one of the best black golfers ever. But he doesn't like that description. The son of an Asian mother and a dad who is a mix of several races, he calls himself a "Cablinasian," the term he invented to describe his Caucasian, black, Indian, and Asian roots.

2   Tiger is not alone. The number of U.S. children in mixed-race families jumped from fewer than 500,000 in 1970 to more than 2 million in 1990.

3   Therefore, the United States decided it was time for the U.S. Census—the government's official population count—to reflect this change. For the first time, in 2000, the census allowed people to select more than one racial category to describe themselves.

4   Every ten years, the census collects information about the people who live in this country. Some Americans argued that racial definitions on the census forms were too limited. Some wanted a new "multiracial" category. The government decided it could get better information by allowing citizens to check off several categories.

5   "Not all Americans fit neatly into one little box," Susan Graham of Georgia told officials who were making the decision. Graham is the mother of multiracial children. She said kids "who wish to embrace all of their heritage should be allowed to do so."

Tiger Woods, one of the world's best golfers

CHECK YOUR COMPREHENSION

Mark each item true (T) or false (F).

_____ 1. Tiger Woods is multiracial.

_____ 2. The number of U.S. children in mixed-race families increased greatly between 1970 and 1990.

_____ 3. Before 2000, the census did not allow people to select more than one racial category to describe themselves.

_____ 4. All Americans fit neatly in one box on the census form.

_____ 5. The year 2000 was the first time the census collected information about the people who live in the United States.

Between 1986 and 1991, the total enrollment in U.S. public schools increased only 4.2 percent. However, during the same time period, the number of students with little or no knowledge of English increased 50 percent, from 1.5 million to 2.3 million. In the Washington, D.C., school system, students speak 127 different languages and dialects. In the California public schools, one out of six students was born outside the United States, and one out of three speaks a language other than English at home. These students, as well as their teachers, face many challenges including what language to use in the classroom. Some people believe children of immigrants should be taught in their native language.

REACT AND RESPOND Do you think these children should be taught in their native language, in both their native language and English, or in English all the time? Why?

CULTURE KERNEL

Over half of the residents of New York City today are either immigrants or children of immigrants.

HISTORY MAKER: Christa McAuliffe

Read the facts about Christa McAuliffe, the mother and teacher who was killed when the space shuttle Challenger *blew up on liftoff in 1986. Then choose the information you want from the list to write a paragraph about her on a separate piece of paper. Be sure to begin your paragraph with a topic sentence that states the main idea. Include transition words to guide your readers from one point to the next.*

- born in 1948 in Framingham, Massachusetts

- received bachelor's degree from Framingham State College in 1970

- received master's degree in education from Bowie State College in 1978

- was high school economics, law, and American history teacher

- developed and taught course called "The American Woman"

- involved in community (Girl Scouts, church, hospital, YMCA)

- was an ordinary person who did something extraordinary

- was a person who took risks to achieve goals

- chosen from 11,000 applications to be first civilian in space

- was astronaut aboard space shuttle *Challenger*

Christa McAuliffe, the first civilian in space

- admired pioneers of the American West
- remembered as modern pioneer
- married with two children
- died January 28, 1986, when *Challenger* exploded, seventy-three seconds after liftoff

Exchange paragraphs with a partner. Read your partner's paragraph and check it for correct grammar, punctuation, and capitalization.

SKILL REVIEW: Summarizing

Read the passage about a famous chess game and complete the exercise that follows.

Man vs. Machine

1   One of the century's most celebrated chess games took place on February 10, 1996, between international chess champion Garry Kasparov and Big Blue, the IBM chess-playing computer. It was the first time a world champion ever competed against a computer in a tournament. It was also an unusual match in that Kasparov lost the first game of the six-game tournament. The games between Kasparov and Big Blue did not take place in the standard face-to-face format. Since the 1,400-pound Big Blue could not make the trip from "his" home in New York to the match in Philadelphia, the players' moves were sent back and forth over the phone lines. As Big Blue figured out his best moves, a technician who was actually at the match in Philadelphia moved the chess pieces. In the end, Kasparov prevailed. He won the tournament four games to two and took home the $400,000 in prize money.

2   While humans can think through fewer than 200 chess positions per minute, Big Blue can sort through more than 20 billion. The elation that followed Kasparov's win in 1996 turned to disappointment when he lost in a 1997 rematch. Kasparov held his own against the computer for the first five games. By game six, however, he was completely exhausted and made a fatal mistake. Kasparov wanted to win. He wanted to beat the machine. He wanted to prove that the human brain can use intuition and imagination to go beyond intelligence. With the 1997 loss, the usual questions arose about the virtue of creating machines that are smarter than their creators. Contests between man and machine have always made us wonder who the real champion is—the human or the machine the human invents. The new question is, if a computer can be programmed to play chess like Kasparov, can it also be programmed to write like Shakespeare?

Write a short summary of the passage on the lines.

_____

_____

_____

_____

_____

_____

_____

PUT IT TOGETHER

Discuss the questions.

1. Author John Elson has said, "From its colonial beginnings, the history of America has largely been the story of how immigrants from the old world conquered the new."[1] Discuss the ways that this statement is true.

2. Does technology help you get away from work or does it tie you more closely to it? Do you find it difficult or easy to forget about your work in order to relax and have a good time? Do you usually take a laptop computer on your vacation with you? What about a cell phone? Fax machine? Pager?

3. If you had six months off from school or work and plenty of money, where would you go and what would you do?

4. Agree or disagree with the following statement: "If you don't know history, you don't know anything."

CULTURE KERNEL

The Vietnam Veterans Memorial is the most visited memorial in Washington, D.C. It was designed by a twenty-two-year-old architecture student named Maya Lin.

The Vietnam War Memorial in Washington D.C.

---

[1]John Elson, "The Great Migration," *Time,* Fall Special Issue, 1993, 28.

PREDICTIONS FROM 1900

*I*n this epilogue, you will read an article

written in 1900 by John Elfreth Watkins Jr. In

his article, he made predictions about life in the

twentieth century. One hundred years later, a

popular magazine reprinted Watkins's article,

along with some thoughts from the editor.

READING 1 **Predictions from 1900**

This article includes an introductory "Note from the Editor," Watkins's original article, and the editor's feelings about the accuracy of the predictions.

AS YOU READ

As you read Watkins's article, compare and contrast the reality of life today with his predictions.

Predictions from 1900
by John Elfreth Watkins Jr.

A NOTE FROM THE EDITOR

In the year 1900, life in America was more similar to what it had been in 1800, 100 years earlier, than to what it is now. "Horseless carriages" were just making their appearance west of the Mississippi.

Women would not be allowed to vote for another twenty years. The Industrial Revolution had already produced many changes, but the age of modern technology had not yet begun. Air travel was considered a foolish dream. The telephone was a phenomenon of modern science.

Imagine the likelihood of someone in 1900 being able to predict what life would be like now—and being at all accurate!

Someone did. He was a thirty-year-old journalist named John Elfreth Watkins Jr. His predictions were published in the December 1900 issue of The Ladies' Home Journal. *Watkins consulted with experts in many fields, then made wide-ranging and imaginative guesses about life in the year 2000. While some things he predicted have not happened—and probably will not happen—he showed remarkable foresight, especially for a person of his era. We should remember that far more change has occurred in the last forty years than most people in earlier times would ever have thought possible.*

1. Five hundred million people. There will probably be from 350 million to 500 million people in America and its possessions by the end of another century. Nicaragua will ask for admission to our Union after the completion of the great canal. Mexico will be next. Europe, seeking more territory to the south of us, will cause many of the South and Central American republics to be voted into the Union by their own people.

2. How children will be taught. A university education will be free to every man and woman. Several great national universities will have been established. Children will study a simple English grammar adapted to simplified English, and not copied after the Latin. Time will be saved by grouping similar subjects. Poor students will be given free board, free clothing and free books if they are ambitious and actually unable to meet their school and college expenses. Medical inspectors regularly visiting the public schools will give poor children free eyeglasses, free dentistry and free medical attention of every kind. The very poor will, when necessary, get free rides to and from school and free lunches between sessions. In vacation time poor children will be taken on trips to various parts of the world. Etiquette (proper manners and social behavior) and housekeeping will be important studies in the public schools.

3. The American will be taller by from one to two inches. His stature will result from better health, due to vast reforms in medicine, sanitation, food and athletics. He will live fifty years instead of thirty-five as at present—for he will reside in the suburbs. The city house will practically be no more. Building in blocks will be illegal. The trip from suburban home to office will require a few minutes only. A penny will pay the fare.

4. Few drugs will be swallowed or taken into the stomach unless needed for the direct treatment of that organ itself. Drugs needed by the lungs, for instance, will be applied directly to those organs through the skin and flesh. They will be carried with the electric current applied without pain to the outside skin of the body. Microscopes will show the internal organs, through the living flesh, of men and animals. The living body will to all medical purposes be transparent. Not only will it be possible for a physician to actually see a living throbbing heart inside the chest, but he will be able to magnify and photograph any part of it. This work will be done with rays of invisible light.

(continues on next page)

5. Everybody will walk ten miles.
Gymnastics will begin in the nursery, where toys and games will be designed to strengthen the muscles. Exercise will be compulsory in the schools. Every school, college and community will have a complete gymnasium. All cities will have public gymnasiums. A man or woman unable to walk ten miles at a stretch will be regarded as weak.

6. Man will see around the world.
Persons and things of all kinds will be brought within focus of cameras connected electrically with screens at opposite ends of circuits, thousands of miles at a span. American audiences in their theatres will view upon huge curtains before them the coronations of kings in Europe or the progress of battles in the Orient. The instrument bringing these distant scenes to the very doors of people will be connected with a giant telephone apparatus transmitting each incidental sound in its appropriate place.

7. Hot and cold air from faucet. Hot or cold air will be turned on from faucets to regulate the temperature of a house as we now turn on hot or cold water from faucets to regulate the temperature of the bath. Companies will supply this cool air and heat to city houses in the same way as now our gas or electricity is supplied. Waking up early to build the furnace fire will be a job of the olden times. Homes will have no chimneys, because no smoke will be created within their walls.

8. Automobiles will be cheaper than horses are today. Farmers will own automobile hay-wagons, automobile truck-wagons, plows, harrows and hay-rakes. A one-pound motor in one of these vehicles will do the work of a pair of horses and more. Children will ride in automobile sleighs in winter. Automobiles will have been substituted for every horse vehicle now known.

9. There will be air-ships, but they will not successfully compete with surface cars and water vessels for passenger or freight traffic. They will be maintained as deadly war-vessels by all military nations. Some will transport men and goods. Others will be used by scientists making observations at great heights above the earth.

10. Aerial war-ships and forts on wheels. Giant guns will shoot twenty-five miles or more, and will be able to destroy whole cities. Fleets of air-ships will float over cities surprising enemies below by dropping bombs. These aerial war-ships will necessitate bomb-proof forts, protected by great steel plates over their tops as well as their sides. Huge forts on wheels will dash across open spaces at the speed of express trains of today.

11. There will be no street cars in our large cities. All fast-moving traffic will be below or high above ground when brought within city limits. In most cities vehicles will travel in subways or tunnels, well-lighted and well-ventilated, or on high tracks with "moving-sidewalk" stairways leading to the top. These underground or overhead streets will be filled with automobile passenger coaches and freight wagons, with cushioned wheels. Subways will be reserved for express trains. Cities, therefore, will be free from all noises.

12. No mosquitoes nor flies. Insect screens will be unnecessary.
Mosquitoes, house-flies and roaches will have been practically exterminated. Boards of health will have destroyed all the places where mosquitoes live. The extermination of the horse and its stable will reduce the house-fly.

13. There will be no wild animals except in zoos. Rats and mice will have been exterminated. The horse will have become practically extinct. A few horses will be kept by the rich for racing, hunting and exercise. The automobile will have driven out the horse. Cattle and sheep will have no horns.

14. Strawberries as large as apples will be eaten by our great-great-grandchildren for their Christmas dinners in a hundred years. Raspberries and blackberries will be as large. One will suffice for the fruit course of each person. Strawberries and cranberries will be grown upon tall bushes. Cranberries, gooseberries and currants will be as large as oranges. One cantaloupe will supply an entire family. Melons, cherries, grapes, plums, apples, pears, peaches and all berries will be seedless. Figs will be cultivated over the entire United States.

HOW ACCURATE WERE THOSE PREDICTIONS?

1. *According to the official government census, there are about 275 million people living in the United States. If we add the populations of Mexico and Central America to that figure, the total is much higher. The great canal mentioned is the Panama Canal.*

2. *Although several billion dollars of scholarship and loan money are available for college students each year, the free college education Watkins predicted has not come to pass. The most expensive colleges today cost about $32,000 a year.*

3. *In 1900, average life expectancy was forty-seven years (not thirty-five as Watkins wrote). Today it is seventy-four years. Although it is true that many people have moved from cities to suburbs since 1900, public transportation to the city costs a lot more than a penny!*

4. *It is true that doctors and scientists have been aided in understanding and treating the human body by such devices as X-rays, CAT scanners, and electron microscopes. So far, though, no one has figured out a way to eliminate pills or needles!*

5. *Americans today are certainly concerned with health and exercise, but we have not yet held our first national Baby Olympics. And it is anybody's guess how many of us could actually walk ten miles without stopping. Could you?*

6. *In some respects, it is true that we can "see around the world." Satellites orbiting hundreds of miles above the Earth broadcast television signals from faraway continents to our living rooms.*

7. *Modern heating systems that use oil, gas, or electricity allow us to turn heat on and off with a knob or dial. But "old-fashioned" wood stoves are still quite popular in areas where wood is plentiful, making wood heating inexpensive.*

(continues on next page)

8. The gas-powered vehicle has definitely replaced the horse for nearly every kind of use.

9. In 1900, Watkins probably was thinking about balloons or balloon-like vehicles when he mentioned "airships." He probably never imagined the large, sophisticated airplanes of today. Watkins was right in predicting scientific uses for airships. He was also right about airships being used in warfare.

10. Military technology has advanced remarkably since Watkins's day. Using computers, radar, and other devices, armies can fire weapons with tremendous accuracy. Missiles can be launched from hiding places underground and on submarines underwater. Some missiles can travel 6,000 or 7,000 miles after being launched.

11. Cities are still very noisy places. Watkins's idea to place fast-moving traffic underground in downtown areas is followed in most cities. Moving sidewalk stairways—or escalators—are now common.

12. In case you haven't noticed, mosquitoes and flies are still around.

13. While it is true that more wilderness land is being taken over by people all the time, there are fortunately still many wild animals on Earth. But a number of animal species have become extinct since Watkins's article appeared in 1900.

14. America is a world leader in agriculture, but our farmers still aren't producing apple-size strawberries or seedless peaches. Maybe in the future.

BUILD YOUR READING SKILLS: Recognizing Main Ideas

Summarize each of Watkins's predictions in your own words.

1. _____
2. _____
3. _____
4. _____
5. _____
6. _____
7. _____
8. _____
9. _____
10. _____
11. _____
12. _____
13. _____
14. _____

EXPAND YOUR VOCABULARY

A. *Match each word from the reading with its meaning.*

_____ **1.** etiquette   **a.** occurrence

_____ **2.** phenomenon   **b.** live

_____ **3.** suffice   **c.** ability to be prepared for the future

_____ **4.** transparent   **d.** be enough

_____ **5.** extinct   **e.** destroy completely

_____ **6.** foresight   **f.** proper manners

_____ **7.** compulsory   **g.** required

_____ **8.** reside   **h.** clear

_____ **9.** exterminate   **i.** no longer existing

B. *Complete each sentence with the correct form of a word from the list.*

1. industrial, industrialist, industrialized, industrious, industry

    a. She is a very _____ young woman.

    b. The environment is suffering from so much _____ waste.

    c. More and more countries are becoming _____.

    d. John D. Rockefeller was a famous _____.

    e. Andrew Carnegie made his money in the steel _____.

2. allow, allowable, allowance

    a. My brother always complains that his _____ is too small.

    b. How much salt is _____ on your diet?

    c. They should never have _____ him to borrow their car.

3. medical, medicine, medicinal, medicated

    a. Always keep _____ away from children

    b. Cough drops should be used for _____ purposes only.

    c. My father graduated from _____ school in 1980.

    d. I prefer to use _____ shampoo.

4. electric, electrical, electrician, electricity, electrify

    a. The lights went out because of a problem in the _____ system.

    b. We had to call an _____ to come and fix it.

    c. You can have either an _____ or a gas oven.

    d. The Beatles _____ crowds during the 1960s.

    e. The _____ went off during the storm.

5. necessary, necessitate, necessity, necessarily

    a. The new law _____ a change in the behavior of young drivers.

    b. The _____ of eating well is obvious.

    c. Expensive restaurants do not _____ have the best food.

    d. If your knee does not feel better soon, it will be _____ for you to have an operation.

TALK ABOUT IT

If you were going to make a time capsule of this year, what would you put in it? In small groups, make a list of the events, movies, TV shows, songs, fads, people, photographs, and whatever else you think should be in the capsule to give future people a picture of life today. Include at least ten items on your list.

1. _____
2. _____
3. _____
4. _____
5. _____
6. _____
7. _____
8. _____
9. _____
10. _____

WRITE ABOUT IT

Write a paragraph describing the ways you think your life will change as the twenty-first century continues.